Henry T. Tuckerman

A Month in England

Henry T. Tuckerman

A Month in England

**ALAN
SUTTON
1982**

Alan Sutton Publishing Limited
17a Brunswick Road
Gloucester

First published 1853

Copyright in reprint   © 1982 Alan Sutton Publishing Limited

British Library Cataloguing in Publication Data

Tuckerman, H.T.
  A month in England.
  1.   England — Description and travel — 1801–1900
  I.   Title
  914.2'0481   DA625

  ISBN 0-86299-020-3

Typesetting and origination by
Alan Sutton Publishing Limited.
Photoset Imprint 10/11
Printed in Great Britain
by Page Bros (Norwich) Limited

PUBLISHERS' NOTE

Although this edition has been entirely reset it retains the spelling of Tuckerman's original.

Whilst the original was not illustrated, the publishers of this edition have included a selection of contemporary engravings to accompany the text.

BIOGRAPHICAL NOTE

Henry Theodore Tuckerman was born into a prosperous merchant's family in Boston, Massachusetts, on 20 April 1813; the son of Henry Harris and Ruth (Keating) Tuckerman. Although firmly American, both by birth and residence, he was the descendant of an ancient Devon family with records going back over four centuries. He was educated at the Latin School and went on to Harvard, but only stayed there two years before embarking on foreign travel as an antidote to ill health.

In 1833 his travels took him to Italy where he discovered a lifelong devotion to literature and art. The next two years were mainly dominated by the country and its landscape and produced publications such as *The Italian Sketch Book* (1835). By the end of the decade, and with his return to Boston, Tuckerman had consciously embarked on his literary career, and in 1843 he tried his hand at editing the *Boston Miscellany of Literature and Fashion*. By 1845, however, he had moved on to New York and adopted a more leisurely way of life which afforded him the opportunity for the quiet study and meditative literary expression which had become so important to him. Here he also made friends with other literary figures, including Washington Irving whose influence shows through in much of his travel writings.

In 1852 Tuckerman paid a brief visit to England, arriving in Liverpool, going on to Chester and from there by train through the Midlands to London. Making the City a centre for a series of excursions by rail he set out to explore 'a specimen of what was peculiar' to England. *A Month in England* is the resulting 'travel guide' – a book for Americans 'with time to spare during the intervals of business or social engagements' and based on the belief that the railway system was so complete that any traveller would be able to visit and thoroughly explore any number of the well-known scenes which he described. Bearing all the hallmarks of Tuckerman's quiet, leisurely style, it gives a fascinating picture of England in the year of Wellington's death and when 'Uncle Tom' fever was at its height with Harriet Beecher Stowe's recent book in the forefront of public attention.

The rest of the '50s and '60s saw the publication of some ten or more other books with Tuckerman taking the roles of poet, essayist, critic and biographer; but perhaps his most lasting work, in terms of reputation, was *America and Her Commentators: with a Critical Sketch of Travel in the United States* (1864). It is interesting that in this view of his native country he should show the same interest in travel which provided the skeleton to *A Month in England*.

In the intervening decade, writers such as Melville and Longfellow had been acclaimed for some of their greatest works, but Tuckerman was well able to hold his own – described by his fellow countryman, S. Austin Allibone, in *A Critical Dictionary of English Literature and British and American Authors* (1900) as a 'gentleman equally admired as an author and respected as a man' and quoted as 'a genial and appreciative writer, combining extensive scholarship with elevated sentiment and feeling'.

Tuckerman was given an honorary degree by Harvard in 1850 and an order of recognition by the King of Italy for his services to Italian exiles in the United States.

He died on 17 December 1871 and is buried in Mount Auburn Cemetery, Cambridge, Massachusetts

PREFACE

So complete is the system of English railways, that four weeks
judiciously appropriated, during the intervals of business or
social engagements, will enable the American, in London, to
visit and thoroughly explore a specimen, at least, of what is
peculiar in the country; he may thus become acquainted with a
large rural domain, a manufacturing district, an ancient castle, a
watering-place, and a venerable seat of learning; and these
excursions will alternate profitably with metropolitan life. It may
seem, however, quite superfluous to record the impressions
derived from an experience now become so familiar; and only
when a new point of view is adopted, can they be supposed to
have any interest for the public. In the present instance, well-
known scenes have been examined chiefly through the medium
of the associations we derive from English authors, and some
new details of local and immediate significance added. If many
of the subjects discussed in these pages, are without the charm
of novelty, it is hoped the light in which they are viewed will
give them, to some minds, more distinct and genial tints.

NOVEMBER, 1853

CONTENTS

CHAPTER I

OLD AND NEW

Hail, Memory, hail! in thy exhaustless mine,
From age to age, unnumbered treasures shine!
Thought and her shadowy brood thy call obey,
And Place and Time are subject to thy sway.

ROGERS

It is easy for a voyager familiar with history and alive to the
ideal, when his eye first discovers the beacon on Cape Clear,
Kinsale or Tucker, gleaming over the sea, to lose himself in the
past of England, and, as he walks the deck alone, summon into
the boundless void around him, shapes of yellow-haired colossal
Britons, Roman soldiers clad in steel, Druids crowned with oak-
leaves, the red-bearded Danish buccaneer, the venerable Bede,
or Dunstan, Alfred and his harp, the dainty Norman, and proud
Saxon, Father Chaucer, Sir Thomas More, Cromwell, the
Merry Monarch, and other prominent figures of English history:
and to intersperse the epochs they symbolize with the eloquent
bards and fair ladies that illustrate each cycle; but when his foot
touches the shore, all such ocean reveries fade away like the
indistinct visions of the night; and the actual usurps the senses
while it breaks the spell of retrospective fancy. The days when
Liverpool was not, and Genoa and Venice filled an equal space
in the world's regard, vanish; and he treads the streets of that
busy haven with no more consciousness of antiquity than New
York of Leghorn inspire; and yet the transatlantic pilgrim
naturally craves the hoary emblems of ages, whose chronicle he
has pondered beside virgin forests; and would calm the restless
spirit born of a new and progressive civilization, in the solemn
air exhaled from the monuments of elder times; he needs to
verify, by observation, what he only knows as abstract fact; he

yearns for the mellow hue which age flings over the landscape; and his disappointment is keen when he sees, instead of hallowed vestiges, the identical freshness and activity beyond the deep, with which he has been familiar at home. Here and there he encounters in the domestic architecture, the ware, the shape of a vehicle, or the furniture of a room, traces of colonial objects yet discernible in primitive American towns settled by the English; and a church, with its cracked tablets and quaint inscriptions, bears testimony to a somewhat more venerable origin than the changeful aspect of his native place can boast; but, for the most part, a few local peculiarities in the mode of life, a different type in the journal, or a less gregarious habit in the people, are the only artificial features that attest his distance from the United States. One advantage, however, this scenic coincidence yields; it vastly increases the effect of contrast when he exchanges the modern city which first meets his gaze, for the ancient one, divided from it by only a few hours' travel; and seldom is the transit from new to old, and from the common-place to the romantic, so rapid.

The neutral tint of the edifices in Liverpool, partly the result of cloudy skies, and in a great measure owing to the absence of red bricks and new paint, the substantial costume, robust look, and pedestrian hardihood of the women, and an air of conservative solidity in warehouse, hotel, and street, keep alive the idea of England, which the scene on the quays and in the shops continually dissipate. The names too, which, with truly British pride, are attached to dock, highway, and inn, recalling war-like heroes, and mercantile princes, confirm the vague feeling in the traveller's breast, that he is "a stranger in the land." As I caught sight, now and then, of the pawnbroker's gilt balls — the escutcheon of the Medici — gratefully rose the noble image of their historian, who here won and lost a fortune in business, and yet found both the time and the intellectual energy to identify his name with the highest philanthropic enterprise, and elegant literature. I sought his grave behind the little chapel where he worshipped, and, standing by the mural slab which only records his name and age, I realized how a true enthusiasm for letters, art, and humanity, lifts the memory of their disciple, like a star, far above the oblivious monotony of trade, into the serene firmament of posthumous renown.

Near the remains of Roscoe are those of that bold and conscientious religious inquirer, Blanco White, who breathed his last at the charming residence of one of his friends in the vicinity of Liverpool. I recalled the wide circuit of rites, creeds, and doctrine, which, with the artless wisdom of a child, he confesses to have experienced, and the profound sentiment of religion that animated his heart, under every form of technical belief; I remembered the beautiful sonnet, in which he compares the unconscious immortality of the soul to the stars hid by the radiant day, yet shining on for ever, and visible when the hour of darkness comes; and I felt how justly we forget the conventional distinctions of Christianity, in view of a character imbued with its essential spirit.

It is a singular fact, that the busy scenes, and palpable results of traffic, and the melancholy quietude of death, are the two points of reflective interest in Liverpool; her docks and her cemeteries, are the principal attractions. Nothing in her prosperous mart serves to remind us that the inhabitants petitioned Elizabeth for exemption from taxes on account of poverty — that Prince Rupert besieged the city in 1644, or that the monks once had a monopoly of the Birkenhead ferry: but, looking through the iron railings down into St. James' cemetery, we see the monument of Huskisson, a stone memorial erected by the sea-captains to their shipwrecked brother, surrounded by evergreens — and recognise the fact, that the wealth which has here found a nucleus, was derived from maritime and commercial enterprise. It is a remarkable coincidence, that the basis of Liverpool's importance was the slave-trade, and that by a natural reaction, her citizens were among the most efficient advocates of its legal prohibition.

The city has a pleasant rural vicinage, and a ride among the hedges and villas, besides cheering the eye in winter with many a picturesque lodge embowered in holly and graceful hayricks planted on the greenest sward, and, in summer, alive with flowers, and musical with birds — warms the fancy with the view of Allerton Hall, the tasteful abode of Roscoe, and Wavertree so long the home of Mrs. Hemans. Well may a poet, however, despair of catching even a glimpse of his traveller's castle in the air, while at Liverpool. He treads the dank pavement of Lord Street, and looks around on the panorama of stores, cotton, beer, and coal drays, policemen with glossy hats, flying cabs, sailors arrayed for a holiday, thrusting out their boots to be polished with a comical air of reckless self importance; he winds his perilous track along the river-side, where a wilderness of rigging is painted on a vast background of fog, a black steam-tug meanders through a forest of hulls and spars, hordes of poor emigrants are collecting their household utensils for a voyage, or gangs of muscular draymen are smoking black pipes — amid the clatter of wheels, hoofs, oaths, mariner's songs, and huckster's cries: he dines with a hospitable merchant, and is environed only with all the means and appliances of prosaic comfort; he returns to the Adelphi or the Waterloo, to meet an English sportsman, fresh from the Baltic or Europa, just landing in the hall a champagne-basket full of prarie birds; and he enters the coffee-room to behold the complacent mercantile effigies round the wall, the same old half-excavated Stilton, and a fresh New York journal on the table.

What room is there for retrospection, when steam and electricity thus concentrate the significance of every passing hour, and the products of sea-divided countries? How is it possible to attain any sense of the past when the present is thus omniverous; and what is there in the life and environment of Liverpool to divert the mind an instant from the actual and material to-day? How shall we flit from the new to the old, from modern, commercial, every-day England, to that which we have learned to love through Shakspere? Take the railway for Chester.

The green embankments, private and carriage-like cars, low telegraph-wires running parallel with the track, and affording means of instant communication through its whole extent; and, finally, the grand dimensions and crystal roof of the station-house, are features of modern science, as applied to locomotion, which do not suggest an inkling of the antiquated towns we are about to enter. An excellent preparative, however, is an afternoon excursion to the adjacent estate of the Marquis of Westminster; for there is an almost feudal relation to the eye between it and the little village through which the traveller passes on his way to Eaton Hall. The low, brick houses, with minute and angular window-panes, occupied by the tenantry, seem old dependencies of the pointed gothic and extensive

structure, with its octagonal turrets, fretwork, and battlements; and between the two, like the type of a third estate, rises the lodge and monastic gateway. It expands the mood, also, of the lover of nature, to behold, once more, even a wintry horizon through a wide belt of sylvan pillars, with groups of deer and flocks of pheasants to animate the turf below; masses of ivy relieved against a time-stained buttress, and alternate species of holly and cypress flecking with verdant sheen the level grass-plats. From one of the quaint little dwellings of the old hamlet there emerged a fat dame with cap, kerchief, and petticoat, exactly like those which adorn the figure of Mother Hubbard as it appeared in the specimens of juvenile literature, with Newbury's imprint, before Miss Edgeworth had infused good sense, and Hans Andersen's exquisite fancy into children's books.

Were it not for an occasional gas-light, our entrance into Chester from a scene like this, would have afforded no hint of the age we live in; for, in the early twilight, the rude pavement, lofty castle, old-fashioned costumes of the venerable citizens gossipping at the city-gate — two boys astride a grey, shaggy donkey — the little shops, dim porticos, huge exterior wall, and narrow streets, are more like a small inland city of Italy than an English market-town. In the parlour of the inn was a print of the Cheshire chase, a family bible, and a tea-service like that only beheld at home on the table of one of the historical New England or southern families; and, at the head of the stairs, a massive and moon-faced clock, that looked as if it had beheld generations come and go. The absence of bustle, the domestic serenity, and neatly-served meal, partaken of in a room with the heavy curtains drawn, and the bright andirons glistening in the cheerful firelight attuned the mind for a contemplative ramble; and when I left the snug retreat, walked a few rods, ascended a flight of steps, and found myself under a long, low arcade, high above the thoroughfare, and lined with little shops, such as are seen painted on the street-scenes of a theatre, I felt as if fairly launched into the region of dreams. Nor was the impression for an instant broken during a walk thence to the Water-gate, and round the walls to the Castle.

When beyond the range of shops, that seemed an indefinite continuation of those which stand on the old Jewellers' bridge in Florence, the open country was visible — spread below as far as the eye could reach, and bathed in moonlight. The hour and the elements seemed to unite in favour of the romance of effect which then and there imagination instinctively craved. Slowly, and with a latent fear that all was an enchantment soon to vanish, I moved around those time-hallowed walls, now looking toward Rowton Moor, where the parliamentary army defeated the cavaliers; now gazing at Brewer's Hill, where Cromwell encamped; and again straining my vision still farther to mark the waving line of the Clwydian range, half-veiled in pearly mist. On the flagged walk lay the shadows of bastion and parapet; the swollen mill-sluice gleamed like silver; and, hanging over the bridge at that point, to watch the whirling eddies of foam, as I inhaled the air "made misty by the floating meal," sweetly rose the image of "The Miller's Daughter," which the muse of Tennyson had stamped on my heart. Here and there a broad fragment of the mossy freestone pavement had sunk, or a portion of the thick, low bulwark curved; sometimes, though at long intervals, a single pedestrian approached from a distant angle, passed, and disappeared; the garlands of ivy pendant from the tower whence Charles I beheld the defeat of his army, rustled in the night-breeze; at one spot a heavy covered boat, the counterpart of those seen in Dutch pictures, floated slowly along the canal, propelled by two women, and, as it shot beneath an arch, and cast its huge reflection on the moonlit water, conjured Venice, like a dream of beauty to the mind.

Here I looked down on an old ropewalk, there on an umbrageous grange; now paused to admire the vast and smooth expanse of the unrivalled race-course, which struck the imagination as a Roman amphitheatre, or field for knightly tournament, and then traced the glistening current of the Dee as it wound through fertile meadows. It required no effort of the fancy, in the hush and solemn light, to recognise, by the very outline of the walled town, a proof of its Roman occupancy — the site and plan being exactly in accordance with their ancient camps; or to realize that the twentieth legion here rested after defeating Boadicea; that King Alfred's daughter built these walls; that Harold found within them the hermit's cell where he buried himself after the battle of Hastings; that King Malcolm of Scotland, upon this very spot, rendered homage to Henry II; and that Edward I and his queen here attended mass at St. Werburgh's church, after his successful expedition against the Welsh.

Instead of cold historical traditions, these memories became present local facts. It seemed as if the clang of armour might be heard from Henry of Lancaster's troops mustering on yonder plain against Richard II; or the echo of a psalm sung by the puritan soldiers then floated across the sleeping fields to the army of Charles, besieged, for so many months, in Chester. I scanned the huge proportions of the castle, massive and hoary, which was founded by William the Conqueror; and stood long entranced by a tower, whence a path, thickly bordered with vines and cypress, leads to a similar structure mantled in ivy — the very stone mellow and crumbling with age; and, while absorbed in the illusions thus created, a sudden noise, like the rush of chariots or the hum of a multitude, came on the rising wind. Had the shields of Caesar's legions flashed in the moonshine, or the golden sickle of a Druidical priestess reflected its yellow beam; a procession of cowled friars wound from the shadow of the wall; a band of mounted knights come prancing into view; or the long fair hair of the wife of Mercia's king streamed to the breeze — hardly a start of astonishment would have denoted the marvel, so completely had nature and antiquity woven their spells. No such test of imaginative triumph was applied; for, awakened from my reverie, it was with a feeling of bewilderment that I recognised the locomotive's whistle, and beheld a freight-train whirl by, loaded with coal from Wales!

The next day I found, to my renewed delight, that sunshine and the ordinary avocations of life cannot dispel the antiquated charm that, like a subtle atmosphere, pervades Chester; seen in detail, and with a broad light playing over its compact dwellings and old churches, the venerable still predominates. Indeed, by revealing many a quaint bit of masonry and dusky nook, the effect in this regard is frequently enhanced. We can then read the inscription on the projecting front of a house, dated 1652, and attesting the pious gratitude of the original inhabitant when saved from the plague; we can peer into the queerest little windows, and behold the low-roofed panelled rooms, in which no legend of ghost, witch, or true-love that did not run smooth, would seem incredible. The higher segments of these domiciles so much overlap the lower, that they look like enormous architectural eyebrows, grey and rough with age.

It is, also, a romantic experience to penetrate, with lighted taper, into a subterranean chapel at the rear of a modern store, and, by its flickering rays, decipher half-legible inscriptions, or the sculptures on a font used by the early Christians; and to pause, in wondering conjecture, before an old and blackened façade, or antique portal. The details of these signatures of the past are no less prolific. Monkbarns would have revelled in Chester, without the slightest fear of his theories being dissipated by the practical comments of Eddie Ochiltree, a zealous antiquarian of his own stamp, having made out a plausible case in his attempt to prove the old city of antediluvian origin.

It is a common occurrence for labourers in excavating the soil, or repairing a wall, to light upon the vestiges of Roman dominion, in the shape of altar-pieces, vases, mythological effigies, a chalice, stylus, moulding, or lamp, and coins, that date from the reign of Caesar to the extinction of the empire. It is to be regretted that these local trophies of the past, have not been collected and preserved in a museum, like that which illustrates the antiquities of Brescia. The gigantic skeleton discovered in Pepper Street, and the remains of Earl Lupus, the Conqueror's nephew, found in their leather shroud and stone coffin, entombed in the cathedral for six centuries, with his enormous sword beside him, would have formed grand central figures in such an archaeological institute.

But the permanent aspect and life of Chester are quite as delectable to the artist and the philosopher, as its relics prove to the antiquary. To walk through the town, as was our fotune, on the bright morning of a market-day, is a pastime that recalls Flanders in the prosperous era of the Low Countries, as depicted by her precious corps of genial limners. I remember a grocer's store in Eastgate Street, beneath the dim little porticos, which are justly considered modifications of the Roman vestibule, that struck me as the very ideal of a shop; its snugly picturesque interior would instantly give Dickens or Hawthorne a hint for a story, and might have warmed Sterne into a sentimental episode. The rosy-faced little proprieter was an epitome of material well being, and the way he dispensed a supply of tea and sugar to a pretty housemaid, who gossipped coquettishly as she leaned on the spotless little counter, was like an incident in some old novel, while the arrangement of the savoury commodities would furnish an effective subject to a Flemish painter of still-life.,

As I stood in the gallery, upon leaving this dainty niche in the temple of commerce, the street afforded an equally scenic and primitive view. A coach passed of the form and dimensions familiar to Richardson or Fielding, half-waggon and half-carriage, loaded to the very roof with passengers, representing every class — the field-labourer in his smock and broad hat, the well-to-do country gentleman, the red-faced groom in white top-boots, the squire's daughter with her air of rustic gentility, the military gallant, and poor vicar in his rusty sable and white cravat, grouped amid baggage, pointer-dogs, rifles, and hampers of edibles, as if the characters in some favourite romance had clubbed to go on a picnic. Then came along a brewer's cart drawn by one of those gigantic horses that are seen in the vicinity of the London docks; his chest seemed to fill up the narrow street, as, with the utmost apparent ease, he drew a towering pile of reeking ale-butts.

The costume of many of the inhabitants of Chester, and even their manner of walking accord with the natural language of the place. I never remember to have seen so many old men thoroughly respectable in their look, but glad in garments whose cut betokened at least fifty years back on the roll of fashion, scrupulously neat but somewhat threadbare. They moved along at a most deliberate pace, leaning on heavy canes, and gazing about them with a Rip Van Winkle air. More than once, too, I beheld some of these primitive figures, that seemed to embody a volume of tradition, emerge from a door, set in an ivy-clad wall, many feet beneath the fortified esplanade where we stood; and on the quaint and diminutive portal glistened a brass sign, with its inscription half obliterated; and it seemed as if dramatic unity required that this personage should encounter another, and a dialogue ensue, as if the whole were but the iniative act of a play, whose scene was laid at an epoch long before the invention of the steam-engine and the cotton-gin.

Some patriotic citizen of Chester has been at the pains to compile its chronology; and when imbued with the spirit of the scene, and gazing on the memorials of its antiquity, it is quite a lesson in the progress of civilization, to compare the wonderful events which have there occurred, at successive eras. The first entry is "A.D. 61 — The twentieth legion garrison Chester;" and the last, "1848 — Chester and Holyhead railway opened to Bangor." Between the two events what progress in science, what triumphs of humanity, and how emphatically does each symbolize an era.

It is only needful to run your eye over this record to perceive what marvellous changes have been wrought by time, the diffusion of knowledge, and the influence of Christianity. The intervals between such mortal visitations as pestilence and famine, are greater as we advance; gradually all mention of burning at the stake, and of the stocks and pillory, ceases; an earthquake, conflagration, or freshet, is more usual at last, than a battle, a siege, or a man hung and quartered; a bull-baiting gives place to a field-preaching by Wesley; instead of Welsh freebooters ravaging the surrounding country, we have noted the visit of Cooke, the tragedian; for the item of a parson and his friends eating a goose on the top of St. Peter's steeple, is that of the burning of Tom Paine in effigy, indicative of the last great climax of politics and religion; and for a king and army passing through Chester to quell a rebellion, a concourse of her own citizens entranced by Paganini.

Approaching the cathedral, we found a neighbouring square alive with country-people, and, for the first time, remembered it was market-day. There were groups of hearty dames with their white caps, ladies in humble circumstances dressed in decent black, and a few epicurean gentlemen standing beside the venders of fish, vegetables, hares, and poultry; the whole, framed by the antiquated fronts of peaked houses, and crowned with a venerable church tower, formed a picture which Ostade and Teniers have made familiar. Worthy to preside, as its architectural genius, over Chester, is its cathedral, the stone itself being visibly decayed, and the old Gothic style prevailing in the model. The bishop's throne, believed to have been the ancient shrine of St. Werburgh, the arms of Wolsey carved at an angle of one of the old beams, the extensive cloistral quadrangle, the vaulted choir, the vestry of Norman architecture, and especially the chapter-house, where the remains of so many earls and abbots repose, combine and reflect to the mind all the successive memories in which it has previously revelled. I felt that even the huge bare walls, like those of the Duomo in Florence, were a requisite background for the crowded imagination; the pavement sagged, in many places, like that of San Marco at Venice; the masonry was fretted by the tooth of time; at every step spread funeral trophies worn by the feet of generations; the surplice of the officiating priest, seen through the distant aisle, appeared like a spiritual vestment; and the gorgeous hues refracted from the stained window, fell on shrine and column like the mellow tints of autumn's dying radiance. When, in the midst of such a temple, I looked on the old banner of the Cheshire legion, the past of England — military, civic, and ecclesiastical — rose vividly to my fancy, in all its poetic significance.

There is yet among the inferior clergy of the establishment, an inkling of that heart of courtesy which originally rendered them the accessible companions of the wayfarer and the kind hosts of the stranger. Again and again, I met with voluntary civilities from members of the order incidentally encountered. An instance occurred at Chester. Attracted by the fine willows in the court of the jail, we were induced to ask admission, and found the prisoners just entering the chapel for morning prayers. The service had to my mind a peculiar solemnity, as I listened with earnest sympathy to the responses of the poor outcasts in whose behalf forgiveness was invoked. While subsequently viewing the prison, which bears testimony to the ameliorating effect of modern philanthropy, I was reminded of the latent barbarism of the English character, by the site of some instruments of torture still preserved as relics — especially what the keeper called a female gag, an iron instrument designed to lock down the tongue and chain it in silence; another horrible trophy was a large collection of ropes with which different criminals had been hung. They were all labelled with the names of the victims, their crime, and the date of their execution. Our cicerone exhibited these grim agents of death, and also parts of the dress of the sufferers, with all the complacency of a gallows virtuoso, interspersing the display with anecdotes of hardihood, repentance, ingenious escapes, and other prison lore. The courteous chaplain doffed his surplice for a mackintosh, and invited us to acompany him to the church of St. Mary's, where he was about to perform a marriage service. It is one of the oldest religious foundations in Chester, and was removed by Randal, the second earl, to its present site; its position is elevated, near the Dee, between the Bridge-gate and the Castle, from which it is divided by a fosse. It is built of the same red stone as the cathedral. Beautiful old St. Mary's! how sweetly thy venerable nave, aisles, and chancels, appear in the retrospect; — each marble cenotaph decked with holly, whose crimson berries made even the dusky entablatures of the dead look gay. I recall, with grateful emotion, even the surly old woman who muttered like a beldame as she unlocked the door, and the sheepish annoyance of the peasant-bridegroom at the clergyman's detention while showing us the monuments. Very stark and mysterious looked those effigies of nobility, grotesquely carved in wood, husband and wife stretched side by side, with the obsolete ruffs, hose, and broadsword; and pensively the religious twilight and hoary shrines yet linger in the memory.

Another of the churches to which I turned votive steps is Trinity, which stands on the north side of Watergate Street. It required no little time and patience to hunt up the old verger; but the trouble was amply compensated when I entered. No special architectural beauty distinguishes the interior; indeed, the greater part of the edifice has been restored, and forty years ago the old spire was taken down on account of its ruinous condition. But I went thither because it is the burial-place of that favourite of Swift and Pope, whose preferment was checked by the death of Queen Anne — the gentle, convivial, benign Parnell, who never rallied from bereaved conjugal and parental love, and, after having been a popular preacher in London, and a successful poet, died at Chester in 1717. Johnson's estimate of his genius is expressively characteristic. In his verses, says the rhetorical critic, "there is more happiness than pains; he is sprightly without effort, and always delights though he never ravishes; everything is proper, though everything seems casual." In that quiet old church, the opening lines of "The Hermit," as they rose to the memory, almost spontaneously breathed the elegy of Parnell:

> "Far in a wild, unknown to public view,
> From youth to age a reverend hermit grew;
> The moss his bed, the cave his humble cell,
> His food the fruits, his drink the crystal well;
> Remote from men, with God he passed his days,
> Prayer all his business, all his pleasure praise."

CHAPTER II

LONDON AUTHORS

Whose fame
Lies sepulchred in monumental thought.

SHELLEY

When the pert chambermaid had removed the breakfast-tray, and the clerical-looking waiter poked the bituminous mass in the grate, until it fairly blazed, I looked out of the window upon the doleful line of cabs, with their smoking horses and mackintoshed proprietors, speculating upon the possible locomotive advantage obtainable therefrom in such weather. The statue of Charles the Martyr stood grimly under a perpetual *douche*, and the top of Nelson's column was garlanded with fog. Both seemed to endure the baptism with cynical hardihood; but all thoughts of the hero of the Nile and the regicides, were dissipated by the names on the glistening panels of each omnibus that dashed by the square. "Hampstead" made me think of poor Keats and his walks when the daisies bloomed along the lanes of that suburban retreat, and of Cunningham, Sydney Smith, and Hood, who lie in its churchyard; "Kensington" raised the image of good Mrs. Inchbald in her retirement there; "Turnham Green" revived Goldsmith's joke; "Highgate" suggested Coleridge, and "Sydenham" Campbell; and I caught myself repeating, with emphasis, "What's hallowed ground?" As if to answer the question, the bell of St. Martin's opposite began to chime; and I remembered that in its vault repose, in most incongruous juxta-position, Nell Gwynne, John Hunter the anatomist, Boyle the philosopher, and one of the brothers who charmed the town, thirty years ago, with that most clever *jeu d'esprit,* "The

Rejected Addresses." The organ of locality, warmed by the talisman of these names, suddenly fraternized with imagination and memory, and I resolved upon a pilgrimage to the haunts and homes of London authors. I began to trace, on a map of the city, the silver lines, which, as a web of light, intersect and overlay the crowded streets and dingy buildings of the modern Babel, with the memories of those who thence sped arrows of thought and dreams of romance over the world; and bequeathed intellectual dignity and enchantment to what otherwise is but a vast aggregation of bricks, mortar, traffic, population, magnificence, and want.

Two minutes scarcely elapsed after I rang the sexton's bell at St. Giles's church, Cripplegate, before that personage ushered me urbanely into the aisle. The roof of the building is modern, but the dark carvings on pulpit and choir indicate an age of two centuries. I stood at the altar where Cromwell and Ben Johnson were married; marked the pavement beneath which Fox, the author of "The Book of Martyrs," is buried; and read the inscription on the Lucy vault — a family satirized in the character of Shallow, and which incarnates for everlasting ridicule the sapient justice who would have proved Shakspere a deer-stealer. I examined the quaint old tomb of the historian Speede: and, from a window, looked upon a fragment of the Roman wall — the greatest antiquity of London, hard by the venerable Cripplegate. Over against a pew, a familiar bust marks the spot beneath which are the mortal remains of Milton; and his epitaph is grand in its simpliticy — "The author of Paradise Lost." He and his father before him were intendants of this church. How sublime to the imagination is this otherwise not remarkable temple where that beautiful head was bowed in prayer! I recalled his image as it lay in youthful beauty, one summer afternoon, on the greensward, under the classic trees of the college-lawn, when a fair lady hung entranced above the sleeper, and left a scroll in his nerveless hand. I saw him in his prime, conversing with Galileo, and looking forth, with all a poet's rapture, upon Val d'Arno from the wooded summit of Fiesole. I beheld him when time had silvered his flowing hair, with sightless orbs uplifted, as his fingers ran over the organ-keys, and the calm of devotion softened the lines of care and grief in that majestic countenance. The picture he bequeathed of Eden, fragrant and dewy as creation's morning, the forlorn glory of Satan, and the solemn cadence of the verse that embalmed, in perpetual music, the story of "man's first disobedience," came vividly back upon my heart beside his sepulchre. Stern Cromwell's rugged visage grew mild as his marriage response woke again from the silence of years, and blithely sounded the footsteps of rare old Ben, as he walked again with his beloved, in my vision, up that solitary nave. What a changed aspect bears the world since Roger Williams talked with Milton of the prospects of religious liberty in America, and the latter plead for the freedom of the press; and yet, with all the triumphs of science, the revelations of the bard have lost not a ray of their spiritual beauty; his "high argument" remains in all its original significance; his mighty song wakes the soul to-day as when first its eternal symphony burst forth; his intact career, unwavering faith, and sustained elevation, reproach the sordid and win the brave for ever.

At the little portal under the archway, just beyond Temple Bar, I knocked until an old *custode* silently admitted me into an alley, through which I passed, to find myself, as if by magic, in a scene of quietude and antiquity that ages and leagues seemed to divide from the crowded and busy thoroughfare I had just left; and, as it was Sunday evening, the court resembled an old-fashioned and deserted city excavated beneath the houses of a modern metropolis, and reminded me of the transition from restless and gay Naples, to hushed and lonely Herculaneum.

I threaded street after street, narrow, dim, and silent, paused in diminutive lanes, whose inhabitants, I could fancy, were turned to stone or annihilated by pestilence; here a dimly-lighted terrace, there an old doorway; now a mysterious staircase, and then a labyrinthian recess, awoke ghostly speculations, and recalled thoughts of the early Christians, who prayed in catacombs. The effect was solemn. The peace of the cloister came over my heart suddenly as a vision of remorse, or the memory of love. It was as if the curtain of night had fallen, at noonday, upon the heaving tide of a populous mart.

I wandered over the site of the churchyard paved with broken tablets, and worn inscriptions; and round the ancient church once sacred to the templars, then the property of the Earl of Pembroke, from whom it passed to the knights of St. John, to be leased, finally, to the students of law; within whose walls Selden is buried, and outside of whose choir lies Goldsmith; where Hooker and Usher lectured, Shakspere laid the scene of a play, and "Twelfth Night" was first performed. But not with these associations was memory chiefly busy, there, in the twilight stillness; I could not, indeed, forget that Clarendon, Rowe, Fielding, Burke, Johnson, Cowper, Sir William Jones, and other endeared authors, once had their chambers in the Temple; but I had come hither, allured by the magnetism of Elia's genial picture; and although Goldy's plum-coloured coat, as he paced the now desolate court on his way to Sir Joshua's; and the shuffling figure of the old lexicographer, in his rusty brown suit, handing Madame de Boufflers to her coach, through a gaping crowd, were inevitable reminiscences, I was preoccupied with the gentle boy already given to quaint musing who so pensively described this scene as the place of his "kindly engendure." I sought, with affectionate solicitude, the fountain he made to rise and fall, the antique sun-dial he eulogized; and, with the shadows of night brooding over me as I explored the scene, and the roar of London life audible from the adjacent street, a feeling akin to the superstitious veneration "with which the child

Elia gazed on the old worthies that solemnized the parade before me," evoked the forms of those benches of the Inner Temple, until, like Banquo's posterity, they glided across the terrace which they once had all to themselves — one with a "gait peremptory and path-keeping, his snuff darkening the air;" another, Samuel Salt by name, with "pensive generality" — then Lovel, the creature of "incorrigible and losing honesty," whom Isaac Walton would have chosen to go a fishing with; and old Barrington, or Pierson with his "incapacity for happiness." Their shadowy forms invaded the dreary solitude, and above them seemed to float a pale cherub.

I was startled, as I moved on, after this reverie, with the echo of my own footsteps; and the patter of an old woman's clogs, as she, sole intruder during that nocturnal visit, died away with appalling distinctness. By the light of scattered lamps it was difficult to read the signs; but, at length, I found "Crown Office Row," where Lamb was born and passed the first years of childhood. He calls it "cheerful;" and one can imagine, that on a fine summer noon, as he roamed about the court and watched the watery jet, or grave pedestrians he so vividly remembered, that this venerable and secluded region wore to his imaginative eye a charmed aspect; it was associated, too, with the endearments of home, and the dreams of a solitary boyhood.

I seemed to catch one secret of his genius, as I surveyed the monastic character of the place where his mind first expanded to life and its mysteries: separated thus from the bustling street, environed by objects that were eloquent of the past, breathing the air hallowed by knightly worship and juridical lore — Jerusalem and St. John the watchwords of infancy — how natural that he should grow up unswayed by the rapid current of life, and unimpressed by the material phases of an existence that seemed to belong to another realm. Think of the effect of daily emerging from the Temple into the Strand, and retiring thither as to a nest and domicile. It was a kind of friar-life, consecrated by seclusion, and what he calls "the most elegant spot in the metropolis," to a meditative and individual experience.

This antique quietude moulded his nature to an observant and reflective habit; and, therefore, when he was forced into the world, it was only "to be dragged along in the procession." The transition from Fleet Street to the Temple, was, to my consciousness, like that from ordinary life to his pages; a serene oddity, a sympathetic charm, a dallying with the things of the hour, as if they were given us only as incentives to fancy, or a nucleus for sentiment, instantly takes the place of the executive mood incident to common life. The fevered pulse grows cool; the roving eye settles happily; the unquiet heart is refreshed by the waters that "go softly." As these quiet precincts stand beside the crowded highway — a haven for the musing stranger, attuning his spirit to life's latent significance, Lamb's own words, uttered with such instinctive pathos, or graceful humour, invade the coarse and hollow speech that, in the world's daily jargon, wearies and confounds. Here, then, I thought, his beautiful spirit first awoke, endowed so early, to taste the sweets of ideal love, to revel in the intense humanity of the old dramatists, to stammer out memorable witticisms, to recognise and celebrate the old humanities, and, in the heart of burly, money-getting, matter-of-fact England, weave mellow hues of the past, suggest heroic comfort, and awaken enduring afection for his own gracious memory, and gentle name.

When in Modena I followed the advice of the bard of Memory, and went in search of the palace, "near the Mincio gate," to see Ginevra's portrait; and here, in London, I could not find it in my heart to be less observant of Charles Lamb's genial counsel, who says, in allusion to the "vast assemblage of boys on the London foundation, who freshen, and make alive again with their sports, the else mouldering cloisters of the old Greyfriars," that "strangers who have never witnessed, if they pass through Newgate Street, or by Smithfield, would do well to go a little out of their way to see."

Unmindful of the vapoury pall that hung ominous and thick over the reeking streets, ever and anon condensing into showers, I left my cabman to his India-rubber envelope, and his horse to the bag of corn tied over his proboscis, and hurried through the archway into the vast quadrangle and dusky corridors of Christ's Hospital. On that winter day they wore a sombre look; the rain dripped from every cornice; little pools gleamed darkly in the hollows of the broad paved area; and I felt as once, during a storm, in Pisa, when I took shelter under the arcades of the Campo Santo; only here the architecture was of a heavier cast, and there were no pale frescoes to enliven the time-worn vaults,

nor even a spire of herbage or timid wall-flower, to whisper of
the leafy web that, in softer latitudes, hides the ravages of time.

In one of the school-rooms, on the ground floor, the light of a
coal fire in the huge chimney, fell on the wan countenance of a
solitary boy who, in the midst of hacked forms, black boards,
and scattered benches, was stooping dejectedly over his book. I
glanced through the window, as I passed, at the "kept" urchin,
and thought of the "objectless holidays" of the orphans
described by Elia; but the reverse of the picture was visible a
moment after, when a dozen little fellows ran across the vast
court, their laughter waking strange echoes through the gloomy
pile. Their costume was a long coat of blue cloth secured by a
leather belt, and surmounted by a white collar folded neatly over
the neck; this attire gave them so much the look of a juvenile
priesthood, and so elongated and solemnized their slender
figures, that their childish gaiety seemed curiously inappropriate. As I walked beneath the pillared archway, I read the
tablets inscribed at intervals along the walls; one announced that
no boy could see his friends during school-hours; one designated
the wards of the nurses; and another proclaimed the benefac-
tions of friends, or the merits of stewards.

But that which caused me to linger and muse, was dedicated
to the memory of Master Boyer, whose character has been so
vividly yet inconsistently described by three of his illustrious
pupils. I recalled his "passionate wig," his "storms that came
near but never touched," recorded by Lamb; and Coleridge's
testimony to the "inestimable advantage of a very sensible
though, at the same time, very severe master," I seemed to hear
his scornful voice criticising a theme: "Harp? lyre? — pen and
ink, boy, you mean; Pierian spring? Oh, ay — the cloister
pump, I suppose." De Quincey calls him the greatest villain of
the nineteenth century, declares flogging was his life, and that
Coleridge's admiration of him was a monomania. The truth
doubtless lies between these two extremes of judgement; and
their contradiction may be accounted for by the intensity, both
of gratitude and indignation, with which we revert to those
toward whom the sense of intellectual obligation is balanced by
rankling wounds inflicted on our self-love. The name of the old
master was a spell, however, that revived the images of those
who profited by his classic discipline, for, with all his eccentric
despotism, according to Lamb, he "made scholars." His name is
at least associated with the freshest reminiscences of genius.
Here, I thought, as I looked round upon the old quadrangle and
massive corridors, knots of childish admirers would gather about
the "inspired charity-boy," and listen reverently to the musical
voice destined, in after years, to chant immortal Geneviève, and
reason eloquently of "foreknowledge, will, and fate;" in yonder
angle, perhaps, sat the kind soul, Lamb's old relative, to bestow
on her darling "the extraordinary slice of bread and butter from
the hot loaf of the Temple;" and by her side stood the grateful
boy, inwardly struggling between hunger and generosity, his
pale features lit up with expectancy, and "contending passions at
the unfolding."

In that chamber, perchance, whose ancient window overlooks
this broad arena, the devout Baxter expired; over these wet
stones the youthful Addison sped to his recitation, meditating,
as he walked, a Latin epigram, lighting with his smile the
gloomy shadow of this vestibule, jovial Steele threw his arm
caressingly over the shoulders of his comrade, and, in the
twilight nook of the opposite porch, Leigh Hunt dreamed many
an Arabian tale. Stillingfleet practised his first rhetoric,

Blackstone felt, on his palm, the majesty of offended law, and Richardson caught his earliest dramatic glimpses of life touched by the mellow hue of sentiment — afterward to expand in "Clarissa Harlowe" — here, amid the sports, lessons, and monastic seclusion of Christ's Hospital. In historical, not less than personal association, is the edifice rich and impressive: the greater part of the victims of the plague were buried there, in the reign of the third Edward. Kings, nobles, friars, pensioners, and charity boys, have had their dwelling-place here in succession; every variety of human character, from Wesley to Tooke, and from Barrow to Camden, have here imbibed the milk of knowledge; and, as I invoked the forms of the departed, a throng consecrated by genius, piety, or adventure, gathered to my mind's eye, in every gallery and over the hollow square, until a vision as glorious as ever filled the brain of the opium-eater, of whose school-days also this was the scene, irradiated the venerable and lonely cloisters.

Gazing up at the enormous roof, I thought of the donkey secretly tethered there, for whom the schoolboy-tyrant (made eternally infamous by "Elia's" record) kept bread from his younger companions; and, in their lofty dining hall, "hung round with pictures by Verrio, Lely, and others," I wondered if blue and tasteless milk porridge was still the order of the day for Monday, and mutton scrags on Friday; I would almost taste the smack of ginger and cinnamon which there endeared millet to the then unsophisticated palate of the child, who was indeed "father of the man," and reverted to his boyhood, with a moral zest indicative of its perennial quality. I looked into the faces of the crowd of blue-coated urchins, then listening to "grace after meat," and would fain have asked if there were yet among them a young stork like him immortalized in the "Recollections," as a martyr to the imputation of meanness, while starving himself to feed his parents. I longed too to recognise Master Matthew Field, that rare combination of "gentleman, scholar, and Christian," whom his quaint pupil so loved to honour; and above all, by slow degrees, yet with a clear and palpable impression, there stole upon me, as it were, the very atmosphere wherein was lapped the boyhood of Charles Lamb.

As I felt in the Temple his infant environment, here came home to me the spirit of his school experience. I realized how the traditional mysteries of these old cloisters aided his dawning imagination; how he felt a peculiar dignity from the "magnitude of the body" to which, at so tender an age, he was bound; and how the sentiment of the past was breathed into his soul from being thus allied to one of its monuments. It seemed to me, then, quite natural that, from such a school, boys should go in search of Quarles' island. I felt no surprise that a noble sense of relation to the great world, should grow up among children already predestined to the navy and the church; nor that the Grecians and the sea-boys were arrayed to the eyes of their gentle brother, the poor annuitant to be, with prophetic interest. I watched the "young monks" through the lens of Lamb's sympathy, and all the effect of "substituted paternity," of "no bills," of "the civic pleasantries of the dispensing aldermen," and "the prescriptive title of admission to the lions of the Tower," in lending a sacred importance to the bluecoat boy of Christ's, was thus fully realized. I thought too, of the boy Elia lying awake in some part of this vast building, listening to the Christmas carol — "transported in fancy to the fields of Bethlehem;" and of his reverent love for "that godly and royal child Edward VI, flower of the Tudor name — the serious and holy child who walked with Cranmer and Ridley — the young flower untimely cropt," and whose effigy he wore on his garments.

From this legendary and sequestered edifice, a short ride transports the literary pilgrim to the scene of Elia's long clerkship. To him the Mint, Exchange (except that De Foe lived many years at its east end), Corn-market, and Bank of England, trophies as they are of wondrous commercial prosperity, are of secondary interest. Cornhill wins his eager glance because Gray was born there; because he tries to discover the shop once tended by the author of "Robinson Crusoe;" and, in the India House, the oriental curiosities will not long detain him from the bust of Warren Hastings, and Clive's portrait, around which seem to vibrate the prolonged echoes of Sheridan's eloquence and Macaulay's brilliant rhetoric. An old porter directed me to the room where Lamb's desk stood. I fancied his diminutive form, arrayed in black, perched on a stool, and his intellectual brow hanging over a ledger. "My printed works," he says, "were my recreations — my true works may be found on the shelves in Leadenhall Street, filling some hundred folios."

How many years of ungenial toil daily beheld this noble sentry at his post of duty, sustained only by the consciousness of fraternal devotion and the anticipation of an evening at hand, when Mary (in the consoling interval of sanity) would sit affectionately at his side, as Wordsworth, Coleridge, or Hazlitt, benignly pour their mental wealth at the feet of her elated brother; or the gentle pair sit cheerily before the mysterious green curtain, while his thoughts wander to that delectable "first play" when the pillars of old Drury shone to his childish fancy, like "glorified sugar-candy." But locality is only the point whence the beams of genius radiate; it is the prerogative of her sacred light that it touches with prismatic hues the familiar and adjacent. The mendicant who pertinaciously opens the cab-door and extends his tattered hat at the crossing, reminds Lamb's admirer of the "Decline of Beggars in the Metropolis;" a juvenile chimney-sweep is an ebony token of his benevolent portraiture; the pallid tailor sewing by the dingy window, excites him to philosophize on the Elia theory of the craft's melancholic habitude; and a Jewish physiognomy revives the doctrine of "imperfect sympathies." If we pass the South Sea House, it is to remember his Claude-tinted daguerreotype of its monitory decay. His quaint diagnosis of metropolitan life haunts his disciple in the thoroughfares of London; and every book-stall hints of treasures in black-letter, and the zest of a long-meditated purchase, such as he chronicled with the garrulous relish of an economical virtuoso.

It accords with the genius of London life that the many taverns frequented by Samuel Johnson, in Fleet Street, are situated at the extremity of narrow lanes, and their proximity only betokened by the glowing letters painted on a lantern which looms upon the bewildered stranger, like a convivial lighthouse through the fog. I passed with utter indifference these alluring signals when they proclaimed the vicinity of the "Old Bell," "The Rainbow," or "The Peacock;" and found there was more in a name than the great bard would have us believe, and that, although a rose might smell as sweet by any other appellation, such was not the case with an inn — at least to olfactories eagerly scenting the haunts of a departed author. But, at the sign of "The Mitre," I startled the policeman whose burly figure, like a flesh butt of ale, nearly filled up the dingy avenue, as I slipped by, and looked through a window hung with legs of mutton, sausage-festoons, and celery, into the earthly kingdom of the author of "The Rambler." The fat landlady eyed me suspiciously through the glass, little imagining that a less material object than the enormous porker behind which she was adding

her score, occupied my speculative vision.

That was, indeed, absorbed with a *tableau vivant* reviving the memorable night when James Boswell, Esquire, found himself familiarly ensconced with his idol, in this to him, as that hour, paradisaical retreat. How eloquently he sums up the items of this triumph of felicity: "The orthodox, high-church sound of 'The Mitre,' the figure and manner of the celebrated Samuel Johnson, the extraordinary power and precision of his conversation, and the pride arising from finding myself admitted as his companion, produced a variety of sensations and a pleasing elevation of mind beyond what I had ever before experienced." Disenchanted at the merely chop-house aspect of a resort which had witnessed those famous colloquies, I hastened to Bolt Court. Here thrift has made capital of tradition, and established a publican's memorial to the famous dogmatist, in the shape of a coffee-room which glories in the title of "Dr. Johnson's Tavern." His cynical squint and heavy wig gleam from the coloured panes; a row of pewter-mugs, and a beer-stained copy of "Bell's Life in London," invite the stranger to repose in one of the snug boxes and talk Johnsonese, meditate on the vicissitudes of authorship, or give his fancy wing over the Happy Valley of "Rasselas." Without this cosy rendezvous, Bolt Court has a forlorn air; two or three brass plates, glistening in the dim lamplight, chiefly evidence that it is still inhabited. I noted, as a coincidence, the sign of a printer.

How often had brave old Samuel tottered up this passage, feeling superstitiously for the posts, and Bozzy picked his way in the rear, with head bent forward to catch droppings of wisdom from the sage. Here he grew eloquent over the tea which poor, blind Miss Williams — fit Ganymede for such a Jove — offered him; and here the Corsican hero, Baretti, and Thrale, have lingered, many a night, for the pleasure of being contradicted; along the adjacent street he carried on his back the famished Cyprian; and thence was borne the corpse of the most heroic of London authors to its last resting-place. That toilsome, diseased, erudite, and devout English philosopher, with his sonorous rhetoric, arbitrary humour, patient taskwork, hatred of the Scotch, and love of Fleet Street, found here a not inappropriate domicile, far away, indeed, from green fields and mountain-air, but near the great stream of human life that he loved to contemplate. The gloom and the individuality of the man were aptly housed in such a crypt, whence, after hours of lonely pencraft, he could emerge, and, in a moment, join the crowd and wend his way to a neighbouring hostel, forgetting, over a joint and can, and with a knot of genial talkers, all mundane things, except the pride of opinion and the comfort of an old London tavern.

To renew his presence in a not less characteristic light, I entered St. Clement's Church (where Nat Lee, the dramatist, is buried), and heard the closing hymn, in the shadow of the pillar against which he was accustomed to lean. With the holy strain, as I looked round upon the worshippers, came the thought of Johnson's reverence — a quality whence arose both the weakness and the elevation of his character, in its blind instinct, leading him grossly to exaggerate the claims of rank, and yield to superstitious terrors; and, in its religious phase, making him solemnly devout. "I shall never forget," says Boswell, speaking of attending service in this very church, "the tremulous earnestness with which he pronounced the awful petition in the Litany — 'In the hour of death and in the day of judgement, good Lord, deliver us!'"

The aquatic birds in St. James's Park, with their variegated plumage, may well detain loiterers of maturer years, than the chuckling infants who feed them with crumbs, oblivious of the policeman's eye, and the nurse's expostulations; to see an American wild duck swim to the edge of the lake, and open its glossy bill with the familiar airs of a pet canary, is doubtless a most agreeable surprise; nor can an artistic eye fail to note the diverse and picturesque forms of the many noble trees, that even when leafless, yield a rural charm to this glorious promenade (the elmes are praised by Evelyn). But these woodland amenities, if they cause one often to linger on his way to the Duke of Sutherland's and Buckingham Palace; and if the thought, that it was here, while taking his usual daily walk, that Charles received the first intimation of the Popish plot, lure him into an historical reverie, neither will long withdraw the attention of the literary enthusiast from the bit of green sward before the window of Rogers, which, every spring morning, until the venerable poet's health sent him into suburban exile, was covered with sparrows expectant of their banquet from his aged yet kindly hand. The view of the park from this drawing-room bay-window, instantly disenchants the sight of all town associations.

The room where this vista of nature in her genuine English aspect opens, is the same so memorable for the breakfasts, for many years, enjoyed by the hospitable bard and his fortunate guests. An air of sadness pervaded the apartment in the absence of him, whose taste and urbanity were yet apparent in every object around. The wintry sun threw a gleam mellow as the light of the fond reminiscence he so gracefully sung, upon the Turkey carpet and veined mahogany. It fell, as if in pensive greeting, on the famous Titian, lit up the cool tints of Watteau, and made the bust found in the sea near Pozzuoli wear a creamy hue. When the old housekeeper left the room, and I glanced from the price-less canvas or classic urn, to the twinkling turf, all warmed by the casual sunshine, the sensation of comfort never so completely realized as in a genuine London breakfast room, was touched to finer issues by the atmosphere of beauty and the memory of genius. The groups of poets, artists, and wits, whose commune had filled this room with the electric glow of intel-lectual life, with gems of art, glimpses of nature, and the charm of intelligent hospitality, to evoke all that was most gifted and cordial, re-assembled once more.

I could not but appreciate the suggestive character of every ornament. There was a Murillo to inspire the Spanish traveller with half-forgotten anecdotes; a fine Reynolds to whisper of the literary dinners where Garrick and Burke discussed the theatre and the senate; Milton's agreement for the sale of "Paradise Lost," emphatic symbol of the uncertainty of fame; a sketch of Stonehenge by Turner, provocative of endless discussion to artist and antiquary; bronzes, medals, and choice volumes, whose very names would inspire an affluent talker in this most charming imaginable nook, for a morning colloquy and a social breakfast. I noticed in a glass vase over the fireplace, numerous sprigs of orange blossoms in every grade of decay, some crumbling to dust, and others but partially faded. These, it appeared, were all plucked from bridal wreaths, the gift of their fair wearers, on the wedding-day, to the good old poet-friend; and he, in his bacheloric fantasy, thus preserved the withered trophies. They spoke at once of sentiment and of solitude.

To concentrate the thick-coming fancies, and hallow the associations of London authors, we must devote hours, when both mood and circumstances are propitious, to their consecrated temple. No wonder that Chateaubriand, wandering in his impoverished exile through Westminster Abbey, became so lost in reverie that he was locked in for the night. The sight of Whitehall and the Horse Guards opposite, if you approach from Trafalgar Square, by recalling the scene of Charles I's execution, chastens the mind for communion with the illustrious dead, by luring it from that tyranny of the immediate, so absorbing in a populous city; and the white vestments of the priests, and thrilling strains of the young choristers, at a distant altar, harmonize with its lonely musing.

To the reverent and sympathetic visitor it is, indeed, a blessing that the jargon of vergers invades not, unsought, the Poet's Corner. Art here does not always keep level with the demands either of memory or imagination; but the very grouping of so many cherished names and effigies, awes the mind with a blended sense of the magic of fame, and the transitory conditions of its achievement. Gay's expression is accordant with his epitaph; we feel that he was one to inspire love. Dryden's bust, like his picture "when younger," at Oxford, is fine; Prior's monument is too elaborate, it savours of the pedantry of the college noted by Johnson; South's mouth and attitude are equally characteristic; Busby appropriately wears the look of a pinched student; Southey is undignified perched above Mrs. Pritchard; Congreve looks Frenchified and artificial as he was; Thomson has a well-to-do air, softened by intellectuality; Barrow's forehead is singularly low; in Addison's statute the face has rather the insipidity of over-culture than the fire of genius, and it is characteristic of him and his times, that he is buried at the side of his patron, Montague.

But special criticism soon gives place here to comprehensive sentiment. What are the rulers whose carved sarcophagi fill the adjacent chapels, to the endeared kings of thought here gathered to their rest? Ideal creations outvie, in such a contrast, the lessons of history. We think of gentle Una and the Canterbury Pilgrims with a deeper interest than the wars of the Henrys and Edwards; Cowper's mental anguish wakens keener sorrow than the heartless espousals of hereditary sovereigns; and "The

Deserted Village" appeals to our humanity more eloquently than Elizabeth's Armada.

The oratory of Chatham, the anthems of Handel, and the portraits of Kneller, have a vital relation to our consciousness; their spell is fresh to-day, while the annals of civic power, typified in the mausoleums of royalty, own but a formal significance. The very names, household words as they are, of this intellectual hierarchy, speak from the cold stone with a pathos and a glory, born only of gifts which outlast all external decay. Verses hoarded in the memory from childhood, recur beside the ashes of those who sang of the changeful seasons, the fallen angels, the delights of fairy-land, and who added to the noble trophies of that dramatic lore, which embalms manly passion in the triumphs of our native language; while the venerable arches, gorgeous windows, and swelling organ, seem to enshrine with kindred forms, hues, and tones, the grand memories they consecrate.

Here, too (though denied by virtue of his meek, and therefore, more previous inheritance in the kingdom of letters, enrolment amid these veteran worthies of the quill), Lamb, ubiquitous to the day-dreamer in London, reappeared, asking, "Is the being shown over a place the same as silently detecting the genius of it?" And again, at Andre's broken monument, I smiled at his Eliaish query to Southey, "Do you know anything about the relic?" insinuating that, made a Vandal by toryism, he had mutilated the figure of Washington; a joke that made the author of "Madoc" cool to his humerous friend for a twelvemonth.

Akin to the epoch of modern literature represented in its social phase by this abode of the banker-poet, the little parlour over Murray's office in Albemarle Street. I felt there, surrounded by the portraits of those, whose writings this famous publisher had first sent forth to charm the world, as if in the very sanctum of prosperous authorship; and, as I compared the lives of these fortunate men with the literary annals of an earlier period, dark with Grub Street privation, fancied in each countenance a smile of complacency; for the spirited face of Byron that here looks down on you, seems innocent of all misanthropy; Scott appears too healthy to worry about his estate, and Jeffrey too good-natured even to provoke a challenge; Crabbe, one could swear, sat for his picture after the complete edition of his poems was paid for; Moore (Sir Thomas Lawrence's last effort) looks as if he had just sung an encored song, and been smiled on by a countess, while Irving seems lapped in his happiest day-dream; only the travellers, Sir John Franklin, Parry, and Barrow, have a look of stoicism, as if they had seen strange things, and overcome great obstacles.

I recalled, as I descended the stairs, that proud day for Murray, when he saw the belligerent authors of "Waverley" and "Childe Harold" reconciled by him, in this very room, go out of it, arm in arm, limping affectionately together.

The sexton had began to extinguish the lights, after Sunday evening service, at St. Bride's, but paused long enough to let me see the altar-piece and the aisle, beneath which lie the mortal remains of the novelist Richardson, and the poets Lovelace and Davenant: three names that revive the fragrant days of early English fiction and verse. It was when living in this neighbourhood, that Milton espoused Mary Powell. I examined the architectural plan of the edifice, one of Wren's early designs, and lingered in the old carpeted vestry, with its venerable portraits, where a group of respectable old ladies were gossipping cheerfully.

I know of no haunts in London more pleasing to a meditative pilgrim than these ancient churches, which, however, deficient in beauty of model and interior decoration, when compared with the religious temples of the continent, have a deeper spell of age and tranquillity from the restless sea of multitudinous life around them, and are usually consecrated to the imagination by sepulchres or registers, which are inscribed with names precious to memory or dear to the curious.

In St. George's, we think of the fashionable marriages with which the romances of high life in England, invariably end beneath that aristocratic dome. St. Lawrence is attractive because Tillotson used to preach there; St. Swithin's, because it witnessed Dryden's marriage; St. Andrew's, Holborn, because Savage was there baptised, and Chatterton buried. As the last resting-place of the gifted, a melancholy charm pervades these places of worship, frequented, for so many years, by the inhabitants of their respective parishes, but seldom visited by the stranger in London.

Even after leaving venerable and magestic Westminster, I could not but gaze with interest upon the more humble proportions of St. Margaret's, for Caxton, Raleigh, Milton's second wife, and Cromwell's mother, sleep beneath. In St. Paul's, Covent Garden, Dr. Armstrong, the medical poet, the author of "Hudibras," whose sarcasms reflect the puritan age, Wycherley, who shows up the levity of the Merry Monarch's day, and Sir Peter Lely, who has left us its pictured beauties, repose together. The cupola of St. Saviour's might serve as a monument to England's dramatic genius, covering, as it does, the tombs of Massinger and Fletcher; and what an era of speculative heroism is suggested in the churchyard of St. Pancras, where Godwin, Mary Wolstonecraft, and Shelley's mother, are buried. Scholarly Akenside, who traced to their source the pleasures of the imagination, may surely claim a passing tribute from the worshipper, with an inkling of that faculty, at St. James church, where his body was interred beside Dodsley, dear to bibliopoles, and good Dr. Arbuthnot, the favourite physician of his contemporary authors.

To realize the materials which London yields the author, we must note the contrast of its daily scenes. In these the dramatists found inspriation, the extremes of condition giving entire scope to every form of passion and element of character. Nowhere in the world, do the two poles of fortune send their magnetic forces so nearly together. The ordinary exigencies of the stranger often carry him, in a few hours, into contact with the most opposite phases of human life — from his banker's in the dusky haunts of the city, to his fashionable visit in the elegant square, he traverses, by the way, thoroughfares where the lowest form of mendicity is seen beside the most brilliant equipages of luxury, and where the struggle for money is displayed in its most subtle, as well as its most desperate shape, from the keen-eyed broker and adroit pick-pocket, to the patient huckster and Herculean draymen — all huddled in one eager mass of keen-scented activity.

There are, however, two scenes which represent so vividly the climaxes of London life, that the English novelists, from Fielding to Dickens, have effectively used them — Hyde Park on a bright Sunday afternoon, and Newgate on the morning of an execution. To the minutest details, these opposite scenes will bear artistic study. As I dwelt on the features of each, it seemed like reading over again some chapter in a favourite novel. The dark, hoary, massive wall of the Old Bailey rose before me like a remembered horror. The dense crowd in the square, even to the individuals, looked familiar. The polished hat-tops of the policemen gleaming in the mist over the sea of heads, pale mechanics and brawny coalheavers munching their loaf or smoking clay-pipes, the cries of piemen, unbonneted and slatternly-dressed women holding up children begrimed and tattered — the talk of Jack Ketch, the veil of fog that wreathed itself over the prison-roof, the occasional swaying of the crowd, the expression of curiosity and hardihood in their eyes — the sudden dispersion and instant recurrence of the usual sound of wheels and voices — the rush, confusion, laughter, shouts, haggard faces, and wet pavement — all were as objects seen in a dream; only when I fixed my eyes on the opposite church of St. Sepulchre (where John Smith, of Pocahontas memory, is buried) did I feel that I was standing in veritable Newgate Street, and not reading a chapter in "Jonathan Wild," or "Oliver Twist."

It was the same walking by the Serpentine. A gentleman on a bob-tail horse, a sort of equestrian incarnation of respectability, I felt authorized to greet as an acquaintance, until I assured myself he was only a character in a book; I was sure two ladies, in a landau, talked to their beaux, who stood by, exactly as the colloquy is set down by Mrs. Gore and Bulwer. I met, at every step, the English aristocrat, snob, and cockney, with the identical costume and air described by Thackeray. The ugly hats, light full whiskers, and smooth chins of the men; the thick shawls and neutral colours of the women on foot; the beautiful steeds and sleek hunting-dogs, the stretches of lawn and clumps of trees, the smoky mirage through which gleamed the sun, making a chiaroscuro that half veiled the line of noble edifices visible beyond the gate; now and then a dowager's heavy coach and fat horses, or a rattling dog-cart, with a rosy girl and her brother, or a snugly-buttoned, middle-aged gentleman, evidently, hastening to a club-dinner, the very canes and grooms, all combined, like the figures and landscape on the drop-scene of a theatre, and were as the interlude between the overture and finale of a piece, the background upon which some dramatic or sentimental interest was soon to develop — an unexpected meeting of lovers, an insult provocative of a duel, or a lively specimen of hypocritical talk between two old card-playing duchesses; some enraged uncle and profligate ward, yellow nabob or handsome officer, parliamentary lion or mysterious foreigner, it seemed to me, ought to appear and enact a part. The stage, and the *dramatis personae,* I recognised, and missed only the plot.

The significant local and social divisions of London life also tend to increase its suggestiveness as a resource of authorship. When the observer can, in so limited a space, become familiar with such entirely diverse forms of humanity, and conditions of existence, as may be seen in the club-houses, each representing a profession, and mark the contrasts between old Jewry and Grosvenor Square, Almack's and Billingsgate, Paternoster Row and Smithfield, Regent Street and Wapping, it is easy to imagine that the intelligent literary artist has characters in every vocation at hand for models. From a twopenny bed-house to the Clarendon, and from the crowd round a puppet-show to a court assembly at Buckingham Palace, the modern author has a free choice of spheres and subjects; and once launched on the tide of popularity, the City and the West-End are alike open to him.

It is comparatively seldom now that dramatic entertainments, in London, repay the trouble of attendance; but the stranger, who looks with disappointment around the vast interior of Drury Lane Theatre, may console himself with some attractive recollections; he can invoke from the dim past the triumphs of Garrick and Siddons, and the social era they adorned; he can speculate upon the memorable night, an epoch in histrionic art, when the pit rose, as one man, to Kean's Richard; he may indulge in graphic reminiscences, of the first representation of "The Beggar's Opera," "She Stoops to Conquer," or the "School for Scandal," all identified with social and literary eras. Mrs. Bracegirdle's charms, associated as they are with the wits of her day; Mrs. Jordan's comic genius and kindly heart; Liston, Munden, Sheridan, Byron; the once vital relations of actor and author, may, to the quickened fancy, lend interest and dignity to the scene of their past glory.

I found it thus a perpetual resource to light up the common-

place scene and conventional manners around, with the unfading
hues of intellectual renown. London Bridge has been modernized, but the walls of the Bishop of Winchester's house, beyond
its southern extremity, yet remain; and within them Dyer,
author of "The Fleece," lived and died, and Sir Kenelm Digby,
while a prisoner, wrote. In Southwark is the site of the very inn
whence Chaucer's Pilgrims went forth. I imagined the scent of
new-mown hay in Little Tower Street, because Thomson com-

posed "Summer" there; in Great Portland Street, I reflected with sadness that the genius or literary hero-worship, in the shape of Bozzy, expired.

Leicester Square was more patrician to my eye, because it had been familiar with the presence, as residents, of Reynolds, Hogarth, Burke, Newton, John Hunter, and Kosciusko — representatives of the whole circle of science, art, humour, statesmanship, and patriotism. Steele used to look out of "The Garter" in St. James's Street, and therefore it seemed more fruitful of humanity; and the coffee-house of the same name I would fain have explored since Goldsmith's "Retaliation" was therein suggested. Crabbe, Moore, Swift, and Scott, I called up in Bury Street, where they used to lodge.

The book-store of Evans was in Pall Mall, and left a charm behind, since it was a favourite haunt of Akenside, Pope, and Walpole. Penn lived at the south-west corner of Norfolk Street, which, in the twilight, methought wore a quaker solemnity; and in Bread Street, where Milton was born, at the same hour, I could almost hear the song — "Drink to me only with thine eyes," for there stood "The Mermaid" tavern, that rendezvous of its author (Ben Johnson), Shakspere, Raleigh, and Spenser. I loved to think of Bacon's Essays when passing under the high stone wall of Gray's Inn, whence many of them were dated; and, in Bow Street, I hailed the traditionary home of Fielding, Waller, and (according to "The Spectator") Sir Roger de Coverley; and it was mysteriously delectable to consider, in Lincoln's Inn, that Cromwell, Sir Thomas More, Sir Matthew Hale, Mansfield, and Erskine, were once enrolled among its students.

In the crowded Strand, how pleasant to remember the boy Coleridge thrusting his hand against a gentleman's pocket while in the fanciful act of swimming the Hellespont — an instance of classical delusion that so won the wrathful man, that he subscribed to a circulating library, in the urchin's name, for a twelvemonth; how charming to think that inductive Bacon and heroic Harry Vane were born there, and that against yonder pillar of Temple Bar, Dr. Johnson leaned one night, going home with Boswell, and indulged in such an unprecedented fit of laughter as to frighten his puritan satellite. Walking, after nightfall, by the cheerful shops of Oxford Street, how vividly

De Quincey's pallid and lofty brow rises before us. Here he first bought opium, and met poor Ann, a hungry wanderer; and subsequently apostrophized that busy thoroughfare as "stony-hearted stepmother, that listens to the signs of orphans and drinks the tears of children!"

At the Tower, who, with a heart in his bosom, does not turn from armour and regalia to the inscriptions on Sir Walter Raleigh's cell, and to the thought of Otway dying at a neighbouring tavern, choked by the bread that came too late? In front of Apsley House, who, with a ray of imagination, does not glance at Beckford's old residence adjacent? Is not Cornhill glorified by the memory of Gray, who was born there, at No. 41? Shall we cross Westminster Bridge, and not think of poor Crabbe pacing to and fro, with his verses in his pocket, the night before his fortunate application to Burke? Or enter Bloomsbury Square, nor try to identify Steele's fine house upon which Addison vainly levied an attachment, to bring his improvident friend to his senses? Or pass through Smithfield, unmindful of Bunyan and Wesley? or Green Arbour Court, and not bless the author of "The Vicar of Wakefield" and "The Deserted Village," who there taught poor children to dance? Is it quite grateful to ascend the old stairs at Somerset House, on our way to the Royal Society, and imagine Cromwell, grim and stalwart, lying in state, and not elegant Sir Joshua Reynolds lecturing on art? Let us ever behold, in fancy, when in Duke Street, our own Franklin, a journeyman printer; in Brooke Street, be haunted by Chatterton's suicide; in the Poultry, imagine Hood, an infant; in Great Russell Street, near Bow Street, do homage to Dryden in his oracular seat at Will's; and opposite, to the author of "Cato," escaped from domestic annoyance, at Button's; let us not return from a party, beneath the stars, through St. James's Street, without a pitiful recollection of Savage wandering there, at the same hour, for want of shelter; and fail not, by way of contrast, in Pall Mall, to moralise on the prosperity of Sir William Temple, near the site of his noble mansion. Let the "Elegy" and the law of gravitation recur to us in Jermyn Street, where Gray and Sir Isaac Newton lived. Let us not despise Hartshorn Lane, for Ben Johnson was born there; nor forget to smile once more at Isaac Bickerstaff's wit, in Salisbury Street, where Partridge the almanac-maker dwelt. It is worth while to say to one's self, in passing Old Bond Street, that Sterne died there, and in Berkeley Square, Horace Walpole; and among the "bachelors of the Albany," as we enter that shrine of celibate luxury, to recall Byron, Canning, and Monk Lewis. Thus, at every step, rise up familiar beings, to solemnize or cheer, and people the memorable sites of London. The variety of character is as great as that of gifts; and the mind is bewildered by the number and contrast of these intellectual almoners, whose bounty is thus recalled where the place that once knew them, knows them no more.

There is a culminating point in national life which is distinctive — an element of the social economy which is ideal, and forms the characteristic interest to a stranger. In Greece, it was especially architecture and statuary; in Italy, it is painting; in Germany, music; in France, military glory; in America, scenery; and in London, literature. Climate and necessity have much to do with this form of human development there. The sensitive and thoughtful are conscious of unwonted pleasure from in-door life, where there is so little sunshine; and the sense of retirement is quickened in the midst of so great material activity. The feel of a carpet, the support of an arm-chair, and the sight of curtains and a fire, possess charms unknown where a gay street population and gardens under a bright sky, make it a sacrifice to remain in the house. Within, there must be resources; where there is isolation, comfort is studied; domesticity engenders mental occupation; and hence the prolific authorship of the British metropolis.

I realized, when housed in London, why it was a city so favourable to brain-work. The exciting transitions of temperature, which keep transatlantic nerves on the stretch, are seldom experienced in that humid atmosphere. The prevalence of clouds is favourable to abstraction. The reserve and individuality of English life, surrounded but never invaded by the multitude, gives singular intensity to reflection; baffled without, we naturally seek excitement within; the electric current of thought and emotion flashes more readily because it is thus compressd; the spectacle of concentrated human life and its daily panorama, incites the creative powers; we are not often won to vagrant moods by those alluring breezes that steal in at our casement at Rome, or tempted to stroll away from book and pen by the cheerful groups that enliven the sunny Boulevards;

and therefore, according to the inevitable law of compensation, we build castles in the air in self-defence, and work veins of argument or seek pearls of expression, with rare patience, beneath the smoky canopy and amid the ceaseless hubbub of London.

Accordingly, there is hardly a street that is not associated with an author; their very names are redolent of pencraft; and how delightful to wander through them unconscious of the heartless throng, oblivious of the stranger's lot, with the heart filled by the endeared images of these intellectual benefactors! The disguised caliphs enjoyed no higher pastime; Aladdin's lamp transmuted not vulgar objects into a more golden substance. We luxuriate in the choicest society, without the drawback of etiquette; we revive the dreams of youth while in the very bustle of the world; we practically realize what a kingdom the mind is, without any technical aid.

CHAPTER III

THE DRUDGE AND THE DUKE

Give up this false idolatry of self,
Which makes your brother nothing.
SCHILLER

Life in England is two-fold: one side is best represented by a process, the other by an environment. The former indicates the secret of her internal resources, the chief direction of her productive labour; and the latter exhibits the most imposing form of her individual wealth. To realize these two significant phases of human existence in Great Britain, we must view them in contrast, and this is done by passing from a manufacturing district to a large rural estate, from the drudge to the duke. All that intervenes between these elements of civilization and extremes of fortune, with the exception of commerce, whose phenomena are best observed at the sea-ports, a careful glance at the scenery discernible even in our rapid transit from one sphere to the other, will reveal.

To an American eye, the most remarkable trait of the land-scape in England is, the comparative absence of picturesque relief; usually a pleasant alternation of meadow, garden, woods, and water, alone diversify the fertile acres. At long intervals only are marked changes visible, and these are rather varied strata or crops than great inequalities of surface. Here and there an elevated strip of land, which we should not dignify with the title of mountain, where rocks and pines give an air of wildness to a highly-cultivated region, is known for miles around as the place to start a fox; but generally, the first evidence of the cessation of a fine agricultural district, is the sight of the shabby and scattered buildings which form the suburbs of a town that owes its rapid growth, if not its existence, to manufacturers; and the canopy of smoke that hangs over its dense buildings, and salutes the visitor with its odour long before the train reaches its destination. The weight of the atmosphere, charged as it is with vapour, not less than the incessant exhalations from innumerable chimneys, occasions this familiar sign of the vicinity of coal-fires. I know not a more comfortless impression than is experienced by the stranger, accustomed to bright skies and a clear horizon, when he first enters one of these scenes of murky toil, on a damp winter-day, especially, there is a forlorn gloom in their aspect, and the very sensation of the place, which makes him realize all the temptations to November suicides proverbial in the land. The idea, also, of human privation, associated in his mind with the locality, visions of famished and desperate chartists, and subterranean labour, haunt the imagination; and it is not until he beholds the brilliant results of forge, loom, and anvil, or finds a social antidote to the atmospheric bane, that his early repugnance is chastened.

The fine shops and nutritive "Albion" of Manchester could not long beguile me; and, as it wanted two hours of the time to start, I determined to see the dwelling of a poet whose very name was a refreshment to the mind in this sooty hive of prosperous activity. It was with a feeling of infinite relief that I rode forth from those dusky and crowded streets, and entered the lane wherein stands the cottage of Charles Swain. Many of his songs, wedded to music by a tasteful composer who once dwelt in Manchester, had been wafted, by their own aerial sweetness, across the sea: and his felicitous description of Scott's funeral, attended by a procession of the romancer's immortal characters, is too graphic a tribute to genius not to be recalled with delight. I entered the family circle — thoroughly English in its geniality — just as they had assembled for lunch. The house is bounded by a snug garden of trees and flowers; the rooms are hung with choice engravings; all around and within indicated comfort and taste; and when I met the dark eye of my friend, I imagined myself in the villa of a cordial Tuscan. The books, the pictures, the hospitable gude-wife, the unaffected and blooming girls, the cheerful old lady by the fireside, and the retirement and quiet thus suddenly encountered, were all the more charming from my idea of noisy, toilsome, smoke-enveloped Manchester so near in fact, so distant in fancy. I was conscious of a peculiar satisfaction at the thought that the poetic instinct could thus isolate a man of soul, whose lot was cast amid the most utilitarian scenes. It was a cheering reflection that, at evening, this brave aspirant could leave behind him the turbid city, and here yield himself to letters, love, and song. How potent is fancy and affection to redeem material life; and how independent are intellectual resources and earnest sentiment of the work-day world! I could readily believe the poet's assertion that the mass of his neighbours had no idea of spirituality except as technically associated with religion; and I honoured all the more the enlightened will, that led him thus to dedicate his leisure to his family, nature, and the Muses. That hour's talk with Swain was a memorable episode in the dreary journey; and I parted with him, at the gate, with my latent enthusiasm carried far above the degree then indicated by the Manchester thermometer.

The glare of the factories at nightfall, the tall grim towers rising in the lunar darkness, the throng of fearless women, the numerous illuminated spirit-vaults, and the mellow sound of the old bells, as they vibrated on the still and humid air, made an effective closing scene, as we proceeded to the station; a mystic stillness and desertion seemed to hang over the moonlit fields, as we were hurled by embankments and bridges, or paused at way depots, crowded with second-class passengers, among whom moved the guards with their flashing lanterns.

The hungry eyes of the beggars as they stared through the windows of the coffee-room at Sheffield, made us hasten from breakfast to Rodger's cutlery show-room, full of steel marvels, whose polished blades were the only brilliant tints observable in the town. Here, again, I sought the residence of a bard. On a hill just without the business portion of Sheffield, dwells the venerable James Montgomery, whose hymns are familiar to the lips of so many worshippers in America. His house is one of a row of neat stuccoed buildings, with a lawn before them, ornamented with trees; the holly and other evergreens looking fresh in the moist air on the day of my visit; from this esplanade the hills appear in the distance, and the city below. The situation is such as a contemplative man would desire, elevated and

with both town and country outspread to the eye, itself
secluded, and foliage and turf around. I found Montgomery in a
snug little parlour, the window of which overlooked this scene;
on the opposite side of the fire his wife sat reading prayers; his
black dress, slight figure, bent shoulders, and thin white hair
rendered his appearance at once scholarly and venerable: with
an aquiline nose and mild eye, he gave me the idea of a gentle
enthusiast, and although he declared himself full of infirmities,
his memory was active and clear, and his interest in all relating
to literature and religion in America, vivid.

The philosophy of labour has never been so thoroughly
discussed as now; and the achievements of science continually
modify the original curse, as the throes of the brain, by yielding
inventive resources, infinitely diminish the sweat of the brow.
One reason why labour in England appears in its most grim and
forlorn aspect is, that little except direct benevolent enterprise
cheers the pale bondmen. Vocation, too, is hereditary, and
seldom progressive. In Italy the climate softens the lot of toil.
Where else can be seen a street-beggar exercising his calling, for
twenty years, in a mood of uninterrupted jollity, like the cripple
on the steps of the Piazza d'Espagna, or in what other region can
the artist find the sleeping face of childhood bland and winsome
as Murillo's infant Christ, with a cynosure of filthy rags, instead
of a halo around it? In the United States, the institutions not
only console but inspire industry. A son of the Emerald isle,
who was my fellow-passenger across the sea, and lunched daily,
in the cabin, on the finest Shrewsbury oysters from his private
stores, was an instance of the prosperous conditions attendant
upon honest toil in America. He had emigrated thither fifteen
years before penniless, and began his career as a warehouse
porter in New York. The savings of this employment enabled
him to set up a huckster's stand in one of the markets, for the
sale of cutlery; and he was now making his twentieth trip, with
unlimited credit on a London banker, to replenish the stock of
his large fancy goods establishment, in which his sons were
thriving partners. It is the want of the hope and prospect of
advancement, that weighs on the heart of English labour. The
native sea-captains at Liverpool see an American sailor arrive in
port one day as mate, then as master, and, finally, as owner, in
each stage exhibiting evidence of improved position and

resources, while they have continued to exist upon the same limited pay, and effected no opening for their children's welfare. In this world there is a vast amount of drudgery to be done, and there will, doubtless, always be drudges to do it; the sad phase of this inevitable destiny is, where the encouragement of a future reprieve, the idea of a progressive experience, is witheld. The only drudges I saw in England with the least satisfaction, were those elephantine horses, with the brawniest of limbs, the sleekest of hides, and the most shaggy of fetlocks, attached to the drays. In the stables of Barclay and Perkins' brewery, especially, there is an array of these noble animals that sublimates the idea of muscular labour. To turn from such to the human drudge, and see a beautiful girl's finger worn to the bone by the process of making steel pens, or a weaver's eyes fevered with rebellious speculation, as he bends such hollow and pallid cheeks over the never-resting loom, startles the coldest heart into pitiful zeal.

The most comfortable of English drudges are the intermediate class, they who act for the producer as brokers and agents. A certain bluff self-importance and shrewd knowledge of the art of getting along, reveals, at once, the commercial traveller. I remember one entered the carriage at Derby, just at nightfall, and the guard pitched into his lap a compactly strapped bundle, which, after seating himself in the best vacant place, he began to unloose. With the woollen shawl it contained he thoughtfully swathed his lower extremities; then hanging his hat above, he donned a cosy little skull-cap; from the pocket of his huge overcoat, he then drew out a small lantern, and attached it, by a hook, to the side of his cushioned seat; having ignited the lamp by means of a lucifer match, he spent some time arranging a little shade affixed to the machine, so as to accommodate the reflection to his eyes; then, with an air of the most cool satisfaction, he took from another deep pocket, the "Times" and "Punch," wet from the press, and composed himself to read for an hour; at the expiration of which time, he extinguished the lamp, and, after several preparatory elongations of arms and legs, laid his red face against the stuffed leather, and nothing more was heard from the dark heap, for the rest of the journey, but an occasional somniferous grunt of animal content.

In Birmingham, where New Street and the Town-Hall proved but temporary attractions, I could find no poet; but, attending service at the little dissenting chapel, where yet worship the religious society to which Priestley ministered, before he embarked for America, I gazed, with interest, upon the tablet there inscribed to his memory, and recalled his scientific triumphs, and undaunted spirit of inquiry.

Here, as elsewhere in the manufacturing districts, the comparative extortion and ill-manners were obvious. The lofty and far-flashing gas-lights loom through the dingy atmosphere like beacons on a sterile coast. Many of the private factories are discovered, after long search, in the upper rooms of squalid houses, approached by narrow and dirty courts; the attempt to gain a true direction from the common people is almost hopeless; they are either stupid, or wilfully misinform strangers; and it is scarcely credible, that such a number of uncivilized beings can exist in the heart of a Christian land. The picturesque costume of the Swiss and Tuscan peasants, the grace of the French bourgeoise, and the intelligence of the poorest Yankee, render the rough, boorish, and sometimes malignant, lower classes of these districts, absolutely repulsive, if not fearful in the comparison. But this squalor and savagery becomes a still more impressive feature to the observer, and a more imperative problem to the philanthropist, from the fact that it is so essentially local. Our way thither exhibited no prophecy of this human degradation; life in the agricultural, and the ancient towns of the kingdom, is not thus perverted; the tokens of social amenities, the memories of national benefactors, and the grace of rural prosperity, meet the traveller at every step, between the drudge and the duke. The journey proves an entire contrast to the arrival.

Scarcely had we left the Euston Station, when again the vivid green of the sward refreshed the eye wearied by the carbon vapour that hangs a brown veil over St. Paul's, and makes dim vistas of the thronged streets. Only the bare trees, and the bleak air, announced the season; and every object wore a freshness of hue and a distinct relievo in the casual sunshine. I gazed, with delight, over a fine meadow slope, at the houses and spire of Harrow, and thought of the reminiscences of juvenility narrated, in mature years, by men known to fame, of which its famous school was the scene; and I pictured to myself the knightly author of "Atala," wandering here in illustrious though impoverished exile, and carrying, through after years, the vision of Byron's youthful head, of which he caught a glimpse at the window.

Along the side of a canal moved a waggon, attended by a rustic, exactly like those which landscape-painters of Sir Joshua's day, introduced into their pictures; the soil reeked with moisture, the clouds brooded heavily, but a wide belt of gold kindled the horizon; a pretty boy, with satchel and white collar, was put into the carriage, by a servant in livery, to go to Dunstable; the shadows of the rooks were distinctly cast on the sward; thatched roofs were seen at intervals, and thus, once more, the most genial and truly characteristic side of English life reappeared.

Then came Rugby, alive with the grateful memory of Dr. Arnold; and soon the fine spires and brick-factories of Coventry, with tints of meadow, hedge, and domicile, as vivid as those which diversify its own gay ribands; a few vagrants were passed in the suburb, to perpetuate the sorry troops with which old

Jack Falstaff bluntly refused to march through the ancient town; and, finally, like a guardian and faithful sentry, rose the venerable cathedral, from whose tower seemed yet to ring the "shameless noon," in honour to Godiva, with her legend revived into more than pristine beauty, in the beautiful paraphrase of Tennyson.

A coach-ride through Derbyshire enabled me to note, with greater precision, the features of the landscape; and to realize anew the beautiful intervention of rustic toil between the drudgery of manufactures and the prosperous freedom of a dukedom. It is in the rural villages of England, that we see traces of her humble life as depicted by Goldsmith and Miss Mitford; and to an American who loves Nature, and her reflection in books, and on canvas, perhaps the most pleasing observation is that whereby he discovers the original sources whence the authors of his noble vernacular and the artists have drawn their memorable themes. Cheerful, therefore, despite a lowering sky, sometimes venting itself in showers, was the view, as our carriage passed swiftly over the broad undulating hills, divided by hedges and crossed by roads where not a stone was visible except those massed in neat, compact walls, or lying broken in heaps to repair the way. Here and there, in the fields, were sheep whose enormous size and large wool-flakes tossed, like the foam of the sea, by every gust of wind, nay, their very expression of countenance, as they looked up from the turnips upon which they were regaling, had a singularly familiar aspect, which I soon traced to Landseer, whose pencil has made the domestic animals of his country as well known as if each stock had been exported. The sparse inhabitants of this well-tilled country, formed a remarkable contrast to the over-populated towns of Staffordshire. At intervals were stone cottages, gray and mossy, mansions of brick, substantial barns, and patches of woodland; the extent of view, and the graceful though unaspiring line of hills, gave to the whole an appearance of rural freedom and prosperity.

A wayside inn, where we tarried, I fancied must have sheltered Morland, or Gainsborough, when caught in the rain, while sketching in this region. The landlady had grenadier proportions, and red cheeks; a few peasants were drinking ale beneath a roof whence depended flitches of bacon, and with the frocks, the yellow hair, and the full ruddy features, we see in their pictures; the windows of the best room had little diamond-shaped panes in which sprigs of holly were stuck; there were several ancient engravings in quaint-looking frames, on the wall; the chairs and desk were of dark-veined wood, that shone with the polish of many a year's friction; a great fire blazed in the chimney, and the liquor was served in vessels only seen, on the other side of the water in venerable prints. It was a hostel where you would not be surprised to hear the crack of Tony Lumpkin's whip, or to see the Vicar of Wakefield rush in, in search of Olivia — an alehouse that you know, at once, had given many an "Hour's importance to the poor man's heart," and where Parson Adams would have felt himself entirely at home.

Soon after leaving this suggestive little inn, we came upon a rocky domain fringed with brushwood, and pronounced a capital hunting-district; then the old signs of cultivation re-appeared, and one village was in itself a picture, consisting of a large group of low cottages, every stone of which was enamelled with moss, and, in the midst, a brown church, with wall and steeple half hid in ivy, and old grave-stones peering from the green turf which smiled around its base; then came fields irrigated by

means of red clay-pipes, in which an old man, with a donkey, was at work, making a bit of landscape such as is often seen in Italy. The gnarled branches of some of the trees, and the patches of gleaming moss upon the dark bark, also contributed to give a look of antiquity to the by-way scenes, not without a pensive charm to the inhabitant of the New World; but this sentiment gave way to one of a more cheerful nature when we entered the villa-like porch, and were seated in the spacious and elegant drawing-room of the inn at Edensor.

The most distinct impression which an exploration of Chatsworth leaves upon the mind, is that of completeness. If the visitor has travelled on the continent, he has beheld statues and pictures as memorable, halls as richly decorated, jets of water almost as lofty, and umbrageous alleys made enchanting by moonlight, and breezes such as are rarely known in England; but nowhere has he witnessed a combination of these and all other resources so entire; and where this unity has been approached, time and neglect have, at some point, trenched upon the perfection of the whole. It is the fresh and thorough order in which every department of the estate is kept, and the miracle of isolating a circumference of eleven miles in the heart of the limited kingdom, and there concentrating all that the wants and imagination of man crave of physical luxury, art, and nature, and thus creating a world for the individual, with the same appointments, graces, and pleasures, that elsewhere, and, by an almost universal law, are the product of civic or imperial enterprise. The fact is still more wonderful to the stranger who enters the magnificent domain fresh from Birmingham and Sheffield. The heart is appalled at the immense disparity of fortune; and a whole universe seems to lie between the drudge and the duke, whose lives are thus breathed out in such startling proximity.

Perhaps the best way to appreciate Chatsworth intrinsically, is to revert to the gratifications we have experienced at wide distances of time and space, and then estimate their concentration here. Think of the hours passed amid the sculptured forms of the Vatican, in the picture-galleries of Florence, of the sylvan zest known in an American forest studying trees or watching deer, of the charm of tropical vegetation, the devout spell of a Gothic temple, the buoyant delight caught from the

sparkling waters of Versailles, the charm of exploring a library
"rich with the spoils of time," the scenic wonders of cliff, lake,
and meadow; and then behold these gems of statuary, painting,
woodland and floral beauty, architecture, lore, and scenery, all
brought together in the most felicitous arrangement of neighbourhood and perspective, available to the senses and the mind,
with the least imaginable expense of movement and attention,
and what a magical experiment it is! The Italian villa, the
English park, the poetry of animal life, the trophies of art, and
the treasures of literature, thus garnered into a single domain,
and that the property of one man, is a spectacle to arouse the
enthusiasm of the poet, to inspire the mind of the philosopher,
and to absorb the casuality of the political economist.

We examine the marvellous truth and nicety of an elaborate
carving of Gibbons, or bask in the mellow tints of a Claude, or
grow reverent before the majestic figure of a Grecian divinity,
and then look through an enormous plate of transparent crystal
upon verdant slopes, marble terraces, a holly-clump whose
emerald sheen glistens, or an Irish yew whose foliated green is
massed in solid proportions, a grove of elms whence an antlered
herd emerge with the confident step of domestic kine, or a knoll,
surmounted with a basin of porphyry, sending up a column of
spray hung round with iris-hues.

The sight of familiar faces gives us a certain home feeling,
even in the midst of this novel grandeur. We recognise, with a
smile of welcome, figures, expressions, dramatic scenes long
known through the choicest works of the burin or the subtle pen
of genius. Thus I greeted, in these magnificent halls, Carlo
Dolce's "Boy," Sasso Ferrato's "Madonna," Newton's "Gil
Blas," Landseer's "Bolton Abbey," the "Capuchin Chapel;"
Joseph at his carpenter's toil, turning to Mary, whose needle-
work is beside her as she lifts the covering from the Divine
Child; Bellini's bust; Aristides, as he stands, holding up his
robe, the ideal of self-respect, in the Museo Borbonico; Canova's
"Endymion," "Lions," and "Hebe;" Teneran's "Cupid," and
Bartolini's "Bacchante." I beheld, in the ferns of the noble
conservatory, the well-known carpet of my native woods; in the
evergreens, fresh trophies of Oregon and California; the
innumerable aloes typified Sicily; the countless variety of palms
revived the East; the bananas and canes proclaimed the West

Indies; and the "hair of Venus" seemed to reek with the damp of Roman catacombs. Reigns, cycles, courts, were resummoned by the portraiture of their heroes; stalactites of Derbyshire spar indicated the geological treasures of the soil; the staircase echoed with princely feet; Pauline's graceful attitude breathed of the palmy days of Napoleon; while the hall of 1662, and the old hunting-tower on the crest of the eastern hill, were eloquent memorials of the primitive life of Old England's nobles, and the bust of Everett symbolized the New England scholar.

It was impossible not to conjecture the receptive ability of the soul in whose mortal name these treasures are vested. If the portraits of the successive Dukes of Devonshire are reliable interpreters of character, it would appear that the first had more fire, the last more benignity; with the gentlemanly air they all boast, is mingled no little complacency, and, in some instances, superciliousness of expression. One would imagine that a look of moral sensibility, born of the responsibility incident to such a heritage, in such a world would pervade their faces. In one point of view, the public spirit essential to character in a position like this, has been nobly manifested by the present Duke. His name is best known in America as identified with improved breeds of cattle, and the triumphs of rural landscape. He is a great botanical purveyor; and it was an auspicious sign that a peasant's buxom wife I afterwards met in the neighbourhood, was earnest in her laudation of the family, whose tenant her father had been for eighty years. The Duke of Devonshire is unmarried; he travels much, and when at home, is courteous, hospitable, and the efficient supporter of the agricultural interest.

If the temptation to linger is the best evidence of the attractiveness of a region, Chatsworth is second to no spot in the kingdom. The inn to which we returned for dinner, presented such a contrast, both in itself and its vicinage, to the recent places of our sojourn, that it was abandoned with painful reluctance. The bright Turkey carpet and snow-white stairs, the airy rooms, rich old mahogany, unexceptionable sirloin, and affable host, with the opportunity of exploring at leisure the noble park, imparted a sense of in-door comfort and rural pleasure without, that it "argued an insensibility" to quit for locomotive restlessness and the spectacle of toil, folly, and crowds; and yet, against this natural instinct for repose in the lap of beauty, there was a protest equally imperative in the prophetic heart, which intuitively feels that only in love and duty is there abiding joy: this compensatory law it is that harmonizes the vast apparent inequality between the duke and the drudge.

CHAPTER IV

A TRIP TO WINDSOR

Thy forests, Windsor, and thy green retreats,
At once the monarch's and the Muses' seats.
POPE

From Waterloo Bridge, the aerial perspective would have inspired Turner. The sunshine glimmered athwart a haze of coal-smoke and vapour, which made the bright tints saffron, and the dark umber; and through this veil, magnified and coloured according to the refraction, were visible the drooping sails of the river-craft, the massive arches of the bridges, piles of buildings on either side; here the bright lines of the new Houses of Parliament, and there the sombre walls of Lambeth Palace.

Quite scenic and picturesque, at that moment, appeared these objects as seen during our rapid transit to the station; it was one of those glimpses which coin the landscape more vividly than a long and meditative gaze, for Nature, the great and ever-working artist, had momently created a memorable effect of light and shade. I could not but deem the view propitious, for it harmonized my thoughts for the day's excursion, and seemed to drop an emblematic curtain between noisy London and the meadow-land we approached; and unlock, by an appeal to the imagination, the fetters of routine, and thus dispose the mind to expatiate in the sphere of the past. This mood, however, was interrupted by the engine-whistle, shrieking echo of a loco-motive age, and those charts of English instincts — "Punch," "Bell's Life," and "The Times." The humour, combativeness, and dogmatism, of these prints, however, had a sedative effect upon the company; and left me at liberty to gaze from the carriage-window, and invoke the associations of the landscape.

I looked down, Asmodeus-like, upon the tiled roofs of Vauxhall, and the trees of its once-famous gardens, and thought of the gaieties identified with the name. A dense mist brooded over the housetops, above which the road is constructed; but when we emerged into the open country, a range of fields met the eye, some vividly green, others inundated; here dark with new furrows, and there laid out in vegetable-gardens, where the cabbages and turnips flourished luxuriantly even in January.

This downward glimpse of a scene where Horace Walpole gossipped, Johnson moralized, and "little Burney" gleaned the material of her once-famous novels, revived the idea of that anecdotical and therefore best-remembered era of London life and literature, which preceded the age of steam. It was refreshing, with the whirling sensation of a railway-carriage upon me, and the proofs at once of the fecundity and superficial character of the press before my eyes, to think of a time when people read with avidity the lay-sermons of Steele, and had leisure to hold long discussions about old authors, and the manners of the day; when men of taste and fortune, like Walpole, took delight in jotting down the social events of the hour, in a style that insured their reaching posterity; and when the authors, statesmen, actors, and artists of the time, fraternized in frank and jovial cliques, with such men as Reynolds, Goldsmith, Burke, and Garrick, for central figures. I could scarcely imagine that these suburban resorts breathed a more genial inspiration to such brain-workers of feverish London, when approached by barge, and the transition from busy streets to rural avenues was more gradual. The comparatively quiet background of life then gave more relief to the individuals who thus represent it to our imaginations. They were neither so widely scattered, nor so lost in the mass, as the thinkers and votaries of art of to-day. There was space enough around each to secure a fresh recognition; and their pursuits so isolated them from the crowd as to make them a galaxy in the social firmament. In the retrospect of our times, the canvas will be too crowded to bring out, in just proportions, the leaders in art and letters; culture has become more diffused, genius less individual.

Here and there, along the road, my gaze rested on the unequivocal signs of a manufacturing district — a row of untidy

brick cottages, and fen-like lands; but, at intervals, came the
true features of rural life — green turf, a sportsman and his dog,
oaks, poplars, and elms, which, although leafless, gave rich
promise of vernal beauty; and, in one field, some mowers were
cutting the barley; while an occasional clump of pines,
cypresses, or cedars, added to the latent freshness of the
landscape.

Then came Putney; and again, as at almost every step around
London, the human began to blend with the local, and yield to
tame scenery the moral picturesqueness derived from the idea of
original character. What varied phases of historical men does the
name revive: here stern Cromwell kept his head-quarters,
elegant Gibbon was born, and noble Pitt expired. How
impressively does the recollection of English civic and literary
life thus identify itself with the view of rural prosperity.

Here a venerable tree gnarled and mossed, there a tawny hay-
rick of symmetrical proportions; now a lane with a footpath
bordered by the most vivid grass, then a hedge impervious to
the eye; and sometimes a meadow of cool emerald expands, like
the plains of Lombardy, in early summer. The landscape was
smooth, well-defined, and fresh, and reminded me of Pope's
muse, to whom it was so familiar — a vital monotony. Near
Staines there rose an old, grey villa, surrounded by poplars,
with walls green from damp, and the adjacent fields partially
inundated, the prototype of Tennyson's "Moated Grange;" and
beyond, we hailed the plains of Runnymede. From a pasture
uprose a flock of rooks, and then alighted, to demean themselves
exactly as Irving described them. A thistle-heath now and then
appeared — undisturbed, because it serves for rabbit-covers — a
significant evidence of that instinct for game which is a national
propensity in Great Britain; and sometimes a grey church-
tower, half-covered with ivy, completed the group of objects
which constitute an English landscape.

Whirled once more in sight of the Thames, it at length wore a
poetical aspect, clear and broad, with sedgy banks, a fine
specimen of villa architecture rising from the smooth lawn on its
shores; and I thus caught, with the first glimpse of Richmond,
the very spirit of Thomson, where he used to lean from his
window to listen to the nightingales, and where Collins bids us
"oft suspend the dripping oar, and bid his gentle spirit rest."

Turning aside from the direct route, two other scenes, dear to poetical memory, allure us — Twickenham and Strawberry Hill. I mused of the bard of society and the virtuoso letter-writer, who came thither to describe what they saw and felt in the metropolis; and to gratify ambition by a masterly though very diverse use of our expressive vernacular: the airy epistle overflowing with details so carefully gleaned and agreeably uttered, that the historian and novelist of our own day find in Walpole the most available facts of costume and manners; and the musical, emphatic heroics, that, like well-attuned cymbals, resound with so many truths of description and character, in the couplets of Pope. Such are the familiar memories that enliven even a winter's day on the road to Windsor.

We look upon a scene remarkably analogous to the authors who so often beheld it; pleasing and fertile, but without grandeur; breathing of plenty and elegance, like the prosperous career of its gifted admirers, with features smooth and fair, only varied by the alternation of the seasons with a look of cheerful repose, few lines of ruggedness, and no trace of sublimity; a scene that, on a warm autumnal day, might inspire such a vision as the "Castle of Indolence," lure a sated citizen to indite a chit-chat epistle to a friend abroad, and induce the mood of patience and elaborate care in which such a high finish of versification is attained as in the "Essay on Man."

A few moments before the speed of the train was checked at Windsor, ominous wreaths of mist that had impended all day, were suddenly dispelled by a light breeze, and the sunshine made every grass-blade and moss-grown bough twinkle. The first view of the Castle was thus auspicious; a beautiful lawn studded with noble elms, across which cloud-shadows fitfully played, expanded to the base of a verdant elevation, and, some distance beyond, rose the grey, compact, turreted edifice, its bold outline projecting from sky and turf, its hoary battlements festooned with ivy, and the banner of England fluttering on the loftiest tower; it realized all I had imagined, and was one of those objects in which nature harmonizes with art to produce a complete effect. This was enhanced, also, by the casual view obtained; and when lost to sight, as the carriages shot beneath high embankments, the image left upon the mind, so venerable, massive, and familiar, conjured from the past a line of sovereigns, around whose titles, clustered events, traditions, and characters, that seemed to group, as it were, in one living picture, the infamy and the glory of the British isles.

Upon entering the outer court, however, on that bright morning, historical associations gave way to the immediate; a little pony-waggon moved across the lawn, in which were two of the royal children, attended by a groom; on the adjacent terrace, her Majesty was walking with a younger scion; the wet ivy on both sides of the window of her chamber, gleamed in the sun; an air of domesticated and rural peace was visible, singularly at variance with the fortified building, and the military guard; and the impression was confirmed as our phaeton coursed down the three-mile avenue, by Prince Albert's farm, where flocks of sheep were browsing, and little brindled cows stretched, with dreamy eyes, on the thick grass. The herds of deer, seen down vistas made by aged elms, the squadrons of rooks wheeling in mid-air, and the cry of starlings, so filled the senses with a feeling of rural comfort and beauty, that it was not until I looked back from the statue of George II, and recognised the towers of York and Lancaster, that the idea of motherly and conjugal Victoria, and her agricultural lord, gave place to the stern vision of Elizabeth and the Henrys.

If a ride in the park, on such a day, enshrines Windsor Castle in the memory as the tranquil and rural home of royalty, a visit to St. George's Chapel during the afternoon service, not less attunes the mind to feel the light and shade which plays over the historical picture. Under the pleasant sky, dark memories would not linger; but, seated in one of the antique stalls of the Knights of the Garter, ushered thither by a verger, with a head bleached by nearly a hundred winters, the tarnished armorial bearings, faded banners, rust-covered swords, even the little brass plates on the old carved oak against which I leaned, inscribed with the genealogy of each knight, whose escutcheon hangs above, and the date of his instalment, some bearing names of historical interest, others known only to modern fashion, some mouldy with time, and others yet bright from the graver, all stir the imagination by the spell of ancient heraldry.

The white-robed canons with their rich voices, a bass and tenor that wake a thrill, especially when followed by the sweet innocent tones of the boy-choristers, chanting an anthem from

Revelation, with the deep vibration of the full-toned organ, combine, in the twilight of the chapel, to win the thoughts far away from the passing hour. On that wintry afternoon, the breath of the reader congealed as it exhaled, and brought to mind Keats' image of the censer, and the old man's prayer, in the "Eve of St. Agnes." The responses echoed through the chill atmosphere. Besides the officiating priests, there were not a dozen auditors; the trophies and elaborate sculptures on the dark wood were only visible by the light of scattered candles; and, at the high window of the Queen's Chapel, I could imagine a fair head bowed in supplication, rendered more meek and earnest by the consciousness of irresponsible power, and the approaching trials of maternity.

One by one, in that solemn air, came out to fancy the kings who were born, revelled, and died in this Castle; the hero of Cressy, John of Gaunt's son, first of the house of Lancaster; the sixth Henry, who founded Eton, married Margaret of Anjou, and who drew his first breath here, and his last in the Tower; his successor, under whose arbitrary yet beneficent reign, Cabot discovered that country whence we make pilgrimages to look on the ancient landmarks of fatherland, even as I then gazed upon this abode of hereditary power then the burly, amorous figure, around whose memory cluster so many fair martyrs, and learned men, whose story is embalmed in immortal dramas, and identified with the beauty of Anne Boleyn, the sacrifice of Sir Thomas More, and the rise and fall of Wolsey; he who broke the ancient chain that linked the kingdom to the Papacy, and united Wales and Ireland to the Crown; the glorious reign of his daughter, with her galaxy of poets and warriors — Shakspere, Bacon, Raleigh, Drake, Sidney, and Spenser; the beheaded monarch whose remains are inhumed beneath the floor of this chapel, where I thus mused; his gay and popular son; bloody Mary who here passed her honeymoon; Anne, with her Marlborough victories and Addisonian wits; the Georges and their statesmen; William the sailor-king; good Adelaide; and now the loved Victoria; here, in the scene of their counsels, banquets and sepulture, their domestic life and rural seclusion, like shadows, yet seemed to hover in the temple consecrated to their devotions and their ashes.

It is the social environment of English royalty that gives it distinctive interest in the retrospect. When Henry VIII is mentioned, we instantly think of Luther and the Reformation; the reign of Elizabeth means the age of Shakspere; of Anne, that of Pope and Swift; Charles I is the prominent figure of a great transition era in politics and religion, to which he was the victim; George III is best recalled through Pitt's statesmanship, as his son, when Prince of Wales, is identified with Beau Brummel, intrigue, and excess, shamefully contrasted with the triumphs of modern science and letters that signalized his own reign.

We perceive why, during the civil wars, this Castle was the most effective military station, and witnessed the bloody feuds which resulted in Magna Charta. Richard II here listened to the charge of high treason preferred by the Duke of Lancaster against Mowbray. It was the last of Charles I's prisons; Cromwell moodily permabulated its walls; and James of Scotland passed within them his long captivity.

These are but a few of the memories that crowd upon the mind, lost in the reveries of St. George's Chapel; but there were two places where the varied associations of Windsor Castle concentrated, as it were, into a more definite sentiment; where the vague annals of royalty assumed a certain individuality; and the scene breathed names that came nearer personal sympathies than those of a long line of sovereigns, who only claimed a thought as the agents of transmitted power, which they used or abused in turn; and at these places I chiefly lingered; they were the terrace near Elizabeth's Tower, and the tomb of the Princess Charlotte. From the one was discernible a landscape that, from the heart of its intrinsic beauty, shed abroad fragrant memories, and the other won regard by the image of a woman who was a sweet exception to the usual career of royalty.

The inconsistencies which attend kingcraft are the best evidences of its want of foundation in nature. Supremacy derived from genius or character is accompanied by the harmonies and unity that proclaim legitimate sway; but assumed greatness based on will, physical resources, or tradition, becomes more and more irrational as humanity develops. Thus St. George's Chapel is dedicated to Christian worship, but the prayers for the Queen, her mother, eldest son, and the Knights of the Garter, by recognising before God, in whose presence all are equal, an invidious distinction even between members of one family, strikes at the root of the religious sentiment, as embodied in the example of Jesus. Not less incongruous is the special petition that the Lord will keep her Majesty "in health and wealth," the forming blessing, which is a natural want, being profaned by association with the latter, which is artificial, and expressly denounced as an end by the Founder of Christianity. A more affecting illustration, of the same kind, is realized when we look upon the expressive mourning figure recumbent over the tomb of Charlotte. Why do all turn, with indifference or disgust, from the mausoleums of the Georges, to breathe a sigh at this sculptured memorial? Is it not because she asserted her womanhood — that, rising above the thraldom of station, she lived and loved as her own nature dictated? Not to the princess, but to the maiden and the wife, in whom regal title could not absorb these more sacred names, is this voluntary oblation paid; therefore, the eloquent Robert Hall pronounced her panegyric amid tears; and the impassioned bard, in his misanthropic exile, broke abruptly from his pilgrimage of song, to mourn the "fair-haired daughter of the isles," who was "good without effort, great without a foe." Her acquirements and charities, her generous and independent sentiments, her love of art and gracious manners, doubtless gained for her a certain popularity; but the rare achievement of domestic happiness in the shadow of a throne, the moral courage that insisted on a marriage of affection, and the beautiful union and simple tastes consequent thereon, combined with her early death, to sanctify her name to the common heart, which always rejoices to behold the human triumph over conventionalism and outward splendour.

A few moments transport us from the tomb of Charlotte to the rampart that overlooks the broad meadows, and glancing river, where the haughty Elizabeth often paced to and fro, chafing, perhaps at the infidelity of Leicester, or struggling with remorse for the persecution of Mary. There is not a feature of the scene, except the stone bulwarks, to indicate the fierce passions that once darkened that lovely prospect. Indeed, we cannot gaze long before the vision of crowns gives place to laurels, and the poetical associations of the landscape veil all remembrance of court intrigue.

Over this parapet Surrey may have leaned. All accounts agree in placing him at the head of the accomplished men of his day. He was educated at Oxford, and travelled in Europe; he early distinguished himself at a tournament in Italy, and at Westminster; a contemporary describes him as "the gallantest man, politest lover, and most perfect gentleman of his time." He married a daughter of the Earl of Oxford. Although the companion of the King's son at Windsor, he lost the monarch's favour, because suspected of having designs on the Princess Mary, and because he is said to have added some of the royal arms to his own; although justified by the heralds, he was impeached and beheaded. One of his effusions, written in the dungeons of Windsor, quaintly alludes to this contrast of his youthful days, and latter fate.

> "When I in joy dyd passe,
> Wythe a king's son, my chyldish yeres,
> In greater feast than Priam's sonnes of Troye,
> Where each sweet place returns a tastfull sower,
> The large green where we were wont to rove,
> With eyes cast up into the mayden's tower,
> And easy sighs, such as folks draw in love."

His manly grace, when on his travels, captivated the nobles of France; and I could easily imagine the rapture that filled his breast, when looking from this terrace upon the far-stretching fields, then covered with luxuriant groves, he was lost in dreams of the fair Geraldine, whom he made "famous by his pen, and glorious by his sword." She was, by universal consent, "the fair;" and was descended from the Geraldi of Tuscany, though born and educated in Ireland; her family were unfortunate, and her mother being akin to the blood royal, she was made the companion of the young princesses. When the Earl of Surrey visited them, in company with the young Duke of Richmond, he became enchanted with her beauty. It would appear that this passion was excited when its object was too young to realize its claims; for her lover says, "She wanted years to understand the grief that he did feel." Fair Geraldine must have had a spice of coquetry in her disposition; but this does not obscure the brightness and depth of her knight's attachment, which was chivalric, sincere, and poetical. When abroad, a famous necromancer revealed her to him, in a magic glass, lying on a couch, with dishevelled hair, reading one of his sonnets. She has been identified as Lady Fitzgerald; and her praise, as sung by Henry Howard, Earl of Surrey, is associated with the earliest specimens of English verse. The victim of a suspicious tyrant, this Castle, where he had moved with the proudest of the land, became his prison. "Windsor," he wrote, "alas, doth chase me from her sight."

Quaint as are the terms of his amorous strain, and obsolete as are many of his words, there is genuine sentiment and beautiful expression in Surrey's poems. Barry Cornwall says he was the first writer of narrative blank verse in the language. He gained high reputation at the battle of Flodden Field. There was a pensive sweetness in the memory of this hero, lover, and poet, who once haunted the park and battlements around me, and, when shut out from these, mused fondly of her who consecrated them to his imagination. I recalled his image in the flush of youth, as here, in the embrace of Nature, he gave scope to a love-kindled fancy; and then, beholding the noble survivors of the forest, whose shadows were broadcast on the level turf, I reverted to the great poet who succeeded, and left the traces of his rich humour upon this very lawn; and the feeble but gifted boy who, at a later period, celebrated, with his precious muse, these noble elms; I thought of Shakspere and Pope. Hither was Falstaff fetched in the basket, and Herne's Oak was his trysting-place; while the juvenile bard's versification, allegory, and mythological allusions, the laudation of Queen Anne, the praise of Denham, the dedication to Lord Lansdowne, and the prophecy of British greatness, render Pope's "Windsor Forest," although the work of a mere youth, entirely characteristic both of the age and the author. It was pleasant to repeat the opening lines on the spot they describe:–

> "Thy forests, Windsor, and thy green retreats,
> At once the monarch's and the Muses' seats,"

and then to compare the still graphic picture:–

> "Here waving groves a chequered scene display,
> And part admit and part exclude the day;
> As some coy nymph her lover's warm address
> Not quite indulges nor can quite repress;

> There interspersed in lawns and opening glade,
> Here trees arise that shun each other's shade;
> Here in full light russet plains extend,
> There, wrapped in clouds, the bluish hills ascend."

A more thoughtful and not less finished minstrel was recalled by the spire of the church at Stoke, rising in the distance, beside the churchyard which inspired Gray's "Elegy;" and his ode on a "Prospect of Eton College" was re-echoed by the sight of its antique towers, "that crown the watery glade," a phrase I fully appreciated as the half-inundated fields glistened with pools:

> "Ye distant spires, ye antique towers,
>   That crown the watery glade,
> Where grateful Science still adores
>   Her Henry's holy shade;
> And ye that from the stately brow
> Of Windsor's height, the expanse below
> Of grove, of lawn, of mead survey,
> Whose turf, whose shade, whose flowers among,
> Wanders the hoary Thames along
> His silver winding way.
>
> "Ah, happy hills! ah, pleasing shade!
>   Ah, fields beloved in vain,
> Where once my careless childhood strayed,
>   A stranger yet to pain!
> I feel the gales that from ye blow
> A momentary bliss bestow,
> As waving fresh their gladsome wing,
> My weary soul they seem to soothe,
> To breathe a second spring."

I know of no sensation, or rather, mood, that so lifts the soul into a region of elevated sympathies as thus reproducing the experience of a gifted mind, in view of the very objects that awakened it. I now felt these gales, and looked from Windsor's heights upon the fertile expanse below, and saw the church beside which those "rude forefathers of the hamlet sleep," whose elegy the gallant Wolfe repeated on the night he was rowed beneath the batteries of Quebec, on whose height at dawn he was to lay down his life, and whose solemn music cheered the last moments of our own Webster; — and it seemed to me like an actualized dream.

An adept in history and architecture, I thought, in looking back upon the Castle, can read in this pile the traces of each reign. The very names of the towers suggest an epoch. Imagine the park in the leafy splendour of June, and then let those whose fate is identified with the scene, pass before the fancy. Through yonder glade, on a beautiful white palfrey, moves Anne Boleyn, with a falcon on her wrist, and the yet enamoured monarch beside her, a vision of grace exultant at its brief triumph; as she turns to smile on the capricious king, with what a shudder we foresee that ivory neck girdled by the axe! From this moat looks up the poet-king of Scotland, watching Jane Beaufort as she waves her hand from the battlements, oblivious of his captivity, with love and the Muse for companions. The sleek and wily face of Wolsey is bent complacently toward the workmen engaged upon his more than royal tomb-house. As he checks his mule to give some directions, how little he imagines that the rich sarcophagus designed to contain his body, will, at last, cover that of the hero of the Nile, in St. Paul's Cathedral. With what bitter impatience Prince John spurs his charger through this gateway, at the thought of his concessions to the barons, who defy him from the adjacent plains of Runnymede; and how melancholy is the air of Sir Thomas Wyatt, as he sits under that beech-tree, and thinks of his beloved in the arms of his sovereign. Behold Father Chaucer walking in the grove below, and rhyming to himself, quite unmindful of his duties as "clerk of the works" going on in St. George's Chapel.

The walls in which so many intrigues, festivals, councils, so many kingly guests, noble prisoners, and lovely women have dwelt, rise to view, in new and picturesque beauty, from every part of the domain; an artificial mere, with miniature frigates and temples, occupies the sight of the ancient lake; and, except the absence of a few sylvan monarchs, the natural features of the park are the same as when, at Elizabeth's command, Shakspere made it vocal with the gay laugh of the "Merry Wives."

When Nature and Art thus combine to symbolize the past, it is genius that interprets history; and the sleeping echoes of Windsor Castle stole forth as syllabled in the memorable verse of Shakspere; the calm but earnest protest of Catherine of Aragon, and the dying charge of Wolsey, to "fling away ambition," seemed alone worthy to express, in words, the moral significance of the closing scenes transferred, in immortal characters, to the poet's record. Nor were the mere facts of departed time thus impressively rendered; dark superstitions and radiant fancies by him gifted with a "local habitation," on this spot, were again repeated to the quickened ear of imagination:–

"About, about!
Search Windsor Castle, elves, within, without."

*   *   *   *   *   *   *

"There is an old tale goes that Herne the hunter,
Some time a keeper here in Windsor forest,
Doth all the winter time, at still midnight,
Walk round about an oak, with great ragged horns,
And then he blasts the tree."

The old town of Windsor seems to nestle beneath the majestic Castle in feudal content. As we rattled by the shops, and through an avenue occasionally enlivened by the figure of a Life-guardsman, my dream of the past was rudely broken, to be renewed awhile as I stood within the old quadrangle of Eton College, walked round the ancient cloisters, looked on the statue of the seventh Henry in the centre, and read the names cut in the walls of the corridor. I breathed with incredulous delight the conservative air of a place where so many known to fame were educated.

It is not long that the mind, in these locomotive days, can be absorbed in the twilight of old; the immediate recalls it with an emphasis not to be resisted; and yet, as I wandered back to the inn, a new and more fanciful series of ideas were excited. "A street in Windsor" brought to mind comic individualities. I instinctively looked around, expecting every moment to catch a glimpse of Bardolph's nose. I was tempted to inquire for Anne Page's house, and hoped I should meet Evans, the Welsh parson, or Dr. Caius, the French physican, going their rounds. I fancied that Sir John's chuckling voice reached my ear, as he cried, "How now, Master Brook! Be you in the park about mid-night, and you shall see wonders." As I passed a field where enormous turnips were heaped, I felt how natural were the terms in which poor Slender was rejected: "I would rather be planted quick in earth, and bowled to death with turnips;" and when the smiling landlady ushered me into the best parlour of her neat little hostel, I was on the point of calling her Mrs. Quickly, and asking, with Ford, "Does he lie at the Garter?" for it seemed a thing of course that I should find old Jack, with Nym and Pistol, quaffing ale by the fire.

Methought the gentleman who was calling after the waiter from the apartment below would bawl, in lusty tones, when he appeared: "Go fetch me a quart of sack: put a toast in't." The table, chairs, and tankard might have dated from Shakspere's day, so rich with time was the hue of the wood, and so antique the patterns; but the engravings on the wall, of Victoria and Albert, and the puffing of the engine at the station opposite, too obviously announced the nineteenth century; and the last fragment of my castle in the air disappeared with the maid of the inn, a kind of faded Anne Page, as she gave a roguish toss of her head in pocketing the sixpence, and tripped away.

CHAPTER V

LIONS

It is a necessity of human civilization that the floating capital of inquisitiveness, public spirit, and gossip, should be provided with a nucleus. The social, like the individual heart, requires an object. The magnetism not exhausted by private demand, is caught up by the common interest of the hour. In the intervals of personal occupation, the restless mind seeks a popular theme, and delights to expatiate in the vast world of opinion and sympathy. In the social economy this demand is essential also to financial success; the caterers to the appetite for excitement need a subject as much as the anatomist, either to dissect or to embalm. How could the trade of playwrights, caricaturists, and editors, flourish without lions? The amphitheatres of Rome, in the palmiest of her circus days, were not more imperative in their requisition. The eagerness of the crowds round a shop-window, the absorption of the newspaper-reader, the hushed attention of the pit, and the vociferous disputations heard in railway-carriages and coffee-rooms, are but the daily proof of the need of a lion to give zest and impulse to civic life; and I know of no method which affords a more direct and reliable insight of national character than the analysis of this phenomenon; for its development varies according to latitude. In Paris, the accidental prism made by the crack of a shop window, the striking resemblance of an actor to Bonaparte, or some other fanciful object, answers for the nine days' wonder of an easily amused capital; in America, a personage who furnishes occasion for a grand dinner or military parade, and can be brought into relation to the idea of progress and republicanism, is most available; while, in England, the organs of combativeness and self-esteem, which predominate in John Bull, must be excited in order to realize a genuine lion. During my visit, there were two lions — one an imaginary character, and the other a dead hero — Uncle Tom, and the Iron Duke; and nothing could be more characteristic than the philosophy of their advent.

Perhaps it is their hunting propensity, so largely developed in the English character, which leads them to run their lions to death; in other words, to multiply the forms of the same idea, and reassert the same dogma, until, by a natural reaction, they are consigned to total oblivion, or reduced to a vulgar standard. Few of the minor inflictions are more irritating to a sensitive mind that this unceasing repetition. The senses fairly ache with the monotonous refrain. It is like the infernal punishment of the tyrant who destroyed his victim by single drops of water falling on his head at regular intervals. In vain we try to escape; whichever direction we take, "there is a lion in the way," and, unfortunately, always the same beast. At first he may excite curiosity, perhaps interest, which, if left to work its legitimate course, may not be without practical results; but thrust in our faces every step, dinged in our ears each hour, and intruded under all possible disguises, we at length feel as if possessed by a demon, haunted by a familiar and remember, with unwonted sympathy, the fate of Sinbad and Monsieur Tonson.

A few months before my embarkation, a story had appeared, illustrative of slave-life in the southern states of America. The incidents were frequently exciting, some of the scenes cleverly drawn, and very judicious mingling of humour and pathos introduced; some of the characters, too, were effectively modelled, and the narrative interest was well sustained. Such were the literary merits of the tale, and they are the same which have secured for many fictions decided popularity; but an additional *éclat* attended this novel, if such it may be called.

To elevate negroes and negresses into heroes and heroines was a new experiment; and to expose to the world, as this book professed to do, a monstrous social evil, awakened the ardent sympathy of philanthropists and reformers. These effects were not diminished by the gross exaggeration and caricature displayed in the story, regarded as a picture of actual life. Indeed, the basis of truth was not examined among the partisans who adopted the work as an exposition of American slavery. The appeal it made to the pity and moral indignation of the public, by high-wrought and exceptional scenes of cruelty and degradation, found an immediate response; the intelligent minority alone compared its revelations with facts, or applied to them the test of reason and charity.

The hero of this African romance is a pious negro called "Uncle Tom" — on the same principle that Goldsmith was called "Goldy" — the epithet being indicative of the confidence and affection he inspired. The idea of showing up a social evil by means of an affecting tale, is not new. Two of the most successful instances occurred in this very country where Uncle Tom became an idol: the eloquent invective of the corn-law rhymer has seldom been equalled; and the cruelty of English law has found dramatic expositors; the dreadful abuse of the workhouse system was exhibited, in a way that brought tears and

protests from thousands, in "Oliver Twist;" while the author of "Mary Barton" drew a picture of the misery of the English operative more tragic than the imagination of the uninitiated ever conceived; the inhumanities incident to the two English customs of flogging and fagging have been painfully illustrated in the same way: yet neither Oliver Twist nor Mary Barton became lions. Why was this honour reserved for Uncle Tom? Because he was the type of an evil which England has had the good fortune to cast off, and because he is the symbol of reproach to America. Thus the national pride was doubly gratified by this canonization; and what rendered the apotheosis more delectable was, that its ostensible, and in part doubtless its real motive, was philanthropy. Thus, during my brief visit, Uncle Tom was the lion.

After passing Holyhead, it was useless to gaze from the wet deck, as we approached the Mersey, a mist concealing every object from view, except the beacons, and, therefore, there was a general rendezvous about the fortunate passenger who had obtained the one journal brought by the pilot. Forming a circle around him in the cabin, we listened with the avidity incident to a fortnight's abstinence from that vital commodity — news; and the first item read was, an account of a meeting of ladies, to present a memorial to the authoress of "Uncle Tom." Thus the initiative breath of English air was prophetic of this tenacious companion.

In a few hours I had landed, and after a hasty toilet, descended to the coffee-room, with the somewhat vivid anticipation of realizing Falstaff's relishing hint of "ease in mine inn;" but lo! upon the tea-table, appeared a polished wooden box, with an engraved metallic plate, upon which was inscribed the announcement, that it was a savings' bank for Uncle Tom; or, more literally, a place of deposit for contributions to aid the originator of that ubiquitous personage, "to abolish slavery in the United States." Having succeeded, by dint of supper and "The Times," in banishing, for a while, this eleemosynary token, I was attracted by a strain of vocal music, and approaching the open door, whence the sounds emanated, listened long enough to ascertain that the melody was Uncle Tom's song, "Massa, I can tell you Nothing." The subject now assumed an ominous phase. It began, in the casual absence of society and occupation, to work upon the fancy. The idea suggested itself, that this sable incarnation of virtue and suffering was not to be shaken off.

I began to long for daylight, in order to find in the novelty of the scene around me, a respite from Uncle Tom. At length a resource occurred to me whereby his darkness might be exorcised until bed-time; and I rang for the waiter, and bade him go round the corner and purchase me a new book, something fresh and clever. As he unfolded quite complacently the volume, descanting on its surpassing interest, and immense popularity, I felt confident I should soon lose all consciousness of my ebony tormentor in a volume of the "Caxtons," or a new number of the "Bleak House," when, to my horror, I saw the familiar effigy of Uncle Tom himself, on the cover of his "author's edition." Snatching the candle from the astonished boots, I fled to my apartment; a cake of Uncle Tom soap was lying on the washstand. I retired into the large, four-post, tent-like bed, and resigned myself to sleep; but the nervous excitement into which I had been thrown by these vain attempts to escape the saintly African, of whom I had experienced a surfeit before crossing the Atlantic, kept me awake.

The smoke of the coal-fire, as I watched it through the open curtains at the foot of the bed, assumed grotesque shapes, always, to my excited fancy, having an African type — enormous flat noses, elongated heels, craniums fledged with wool, and colossal lips puffed into absurd dimensions; then from the crevice of a lump, the flame would dance and turn about like Jim Crow, or contort itself after the style of Topsy, or leap across a fissure, like Eliza jumping over the ice-cakes of the Ohio, or splutter like Sambo in his fun with the slave-hunter, or moan like Uncle Tom in his agony; and when, overpowered with fatigue, I fell asleep, it was to dream of these scenes, amid the sultry calm of a dog-day on the Mississippi, on the hot sands of Africa, or surrounded by pestilence in New Orleans. At length, from this haunted and unrefreshing slumber, I was roused by the grey dawn which stole in at the casement, and banished the fevered visions of the night.

While breakfast was preparing, I stepped over to the hair-dresser's, and under his tonsorial operation, was, perforce, obliged to gaze directly forward. The shop had been newly papered, and, with consternation, I discovered that the entire wall exhibited innumerable tableaux of Uncle Tom and little Eva, identical in design with the frontispiece of that once popular tract of Mrs. Sherwood's, called "Little Henry and his Bearer," which an intelligent critic has proved, as far as analogous extracts can do so, suggested the idea of this religious slave.

Almost frantic with the reappearance of this lion, I determined, immediately after breakfast, to change the scene; but had scarcely taken my seat in the carriage, when a farmer and a commercial traveller began an animated discussion as to the probability of a servile war in America as the consequence of Uncle Tom's advent; while a Quaker lady opposite lamented, with ejaculations of pious horror, the wickedness of Carolinians in keeping their negroes heathens. Presently the subject was taken up by an elderly gentleman, in a sportsman's garb, and before we were half-way to London, the book was thoroughly discussed. I then, as on several other occasions, was astonished at the ignorance displayed even by the middle class of English; they were evidently unaware of the geography of American slavery, and imagined the question to be within the habitual scope of national legislation; it was declared that whipping blacks to death was a common sight in the streets of Boston, and intimated that a vote of Congress, like that of the British Parliament which emancipated the slaves of West Indies, was the simple process required to annihilate the institution, with perfect safety to the nation and comfort to the negroes.

I tried to divert myself at the stations by watching the guard and passengers, or examining the lofty glass domes which form so elegant a roof to the platform; but hucksters continually offered the railway edition of "Uncle Tom" for a shilling, and its title and effigy appeared, on enmormous placards, over the book-stalls at every depôt.

As luck, or rather fate, would have it, the night of my arrival, I was induced to join a party for the theatre. We entered the box of Drury Lane just as the curtain was rising. The scene represented the quay at New Orleans; on a cotton-bale was extended a figure clad in nankeen and a palm-leaf hat, with a whip in one hand and a lighted cigar in the other; he was the image of languor and indifference, hardly capable, it seemed, of lifting the long, smoking coil of tobacco to his lips. Suddenly he rose to his feet, moving to and fro with prodigious alacrity, and bellowing forth a rigmarole of Yankee phrases, evidently borrowed from Hill or Hackett, while he flourished the lash over thirty or forty begrimed supernumeraries of all sizes, arrayed in tow-cloth and striped cotton, who hopped about the stage, yelling at each blow, like so many imps of darkness. At the entrance of Uncle Tom — a very fat actor, with a smutty face, whose accent and pronunciation were those of a London cabman — there was a terrific burst of applause; then came the sound of the aspirated vowels and words, such as might have been gleaned from "Law's Serious Call," to which the screams of the grotesque crowd, the twirling of Topsy (a very tall, thin girl, with two breadths of crash pendent from a neck streaked with burnt cork), and the cracking of the Yankee planter's whip, were unceasing accompaniments. Two females in the next box began to weep hysterically, while our risibles and disgust, excited in equal proportions, obliged us to beat a precipitate retreat.

Not willing to lose our evening's amusement, we drove to a minor theatre. There Uncle Tom appeared as the hero of a melodrama, with the novelty of tropical vegetation introduced in Canadian scenery, and Celeste, as agile as ever, doing Cassy in the most intense style of French pantomime. A single act was all we could endure, and hastening to Astley's, we saw Uncle Tom hunted by horsemen until he sank down exhausted at the foot-lights, and died to slow music, just as his companions brandished their knives in triumph over the corpses of a score of whites, amid the bravos of the audience.

It was then proposed to visit a moot court, held in an inn off the Strand, known by the suspicious name of the "Coal Hole." Although with these dark experiences yet casting their shadows over me, I did not relish the black title of this judicial resort, yet willing to see a diversion peculiar to London, and at the same time, escape, as I fondly imagined, the dark lion who had dogged me so inveterately, I acquiesced in the proposal, and we soon found ourselves beside a table in the retired chamber of Nicholson's tavern; several parties were enjoying their supper quietly in the long and rather dusky room; and here and there reclined a solitary individual, with his mug of ale before him, or two fast boys consulting a newspaper as they sipped their toddy.

Presently the chief-justice and lawyers entered in their robes and huge wigs, with bundles of papers tied with red tape, and all the formal dignity and salutations usual upon the opening of a court. One of the pseudo-advocates was the image of Lord Brougham; the natural language of his nose, and the working of his facial muscles, increased the resemblance, which was further confirmed by a studied imitation of the Chancellor's style of address and manner of speaking. The case was opened, after a little skirmishing of wit between the rival lawyers, by the counsel for the plaintiff; and the merry twinkle of his eye, as well as the humorous intonation of his voice, prepared me to expect no little amusement, and the hydra-headed lion was forgotten. Imagine, then, my despair at the exordium:

"Gentlemen of the jury, the case which will be presented to your notice, this evening, is no less important as a precedent than original in the annals of English jurisprudence. You are aware that an individual is now the honoured guest of this kingdom, idolized in the highest circles, followed by the enthusiastic multitudes, the object of absorbing interest to the gifted, and the benevolent, the confidant of even our titled countrywomen, some of whom, I regret to say, in their blind enthusiasm, forgetful of the native modesty which has heretofore distinguished their sex in this realm, have admitted him to their boudoirs, clasped him to their chaste bosoms, shed tears over his past history, and sworn to console his future life; stately dowagers, and blushing virgins, bishops and peers, rich merchants and professional leaders, all classes and ranks have united to do him honour. What, then gentlemen, will you think of the temerity of the man who has ventured to insult and persecute this endeared stranger? I need not anticipate the firmness with which you will visit upon the defendant, in such a case as this, the penalty of the law. Gentlemen, this action is brought by Uncle Tom against Mr. Smith of the Adelphi Theatre, for misrepresenting him on the stage, and thereby ruining his matrimonial prospects with Miss Coutts, his lately affianced bride."

I will not attempt to describe the arguments on either side, the examination of the heiress, or her discarded lover, both of whom appeared in the witness box, the eloquent harangues, the funny dialogue, or the solemn rebukes from the bench. Suffice it to say, that another phase comic enough to upset the gravity of an ascetic, of this Protean theme, was exhibited. We hastened away, and entered the Divan to sup, but had scarcely taken our places at a side-table, when in swaggered three cockneys, vociferously discussing the speeches they had just heard at Exeter Hall, opposite, in which all the illustrations of rhetorical philantrophy had been drawn from Uncle Tom; and I resigned myself to his finale of the evening's adventures, with an absolute conviction of the impossibility of escaping a London lion.

Impressed with the availability of social evils as subjects for "lions," by this success of Uncle Tom, I could not but think how easily they were to be found here. A spicy farce suggested itself as I thought of the innumerable traps to catch a sixpence which, at every step in England, reduce the stranger's vision of her past greatness, and his relish of her present comfort, to a mood of thoroughly commonplace annoyance. before the regalia of her kings, beside the ancient sarcophagi of her buried royalty, in the magnificent temple of her faith, above the sacred dust of her heroes, in the splendid domains of her nobility, upon entering a cab, pew, opera-box, or bath, always and everywhere, a hat is touched, a hand outstretched, and the sentiments of the place, and the rights of the man, made to dwindle into a miserable consciousness, that "to pole about for pence" is the normal life of Great Britain. It may be artistically objected, that a sixpence, not being personal and incarnated, lacks the essential quality of a lion, which is individuality. But, we have only to look at the fine display of rabbits and pheasants at the market-window, or go from a dissenting chapel to a cathedral service, to find a living substitute for the metallic beast.

With all the facts and figures before us relative to the monopoly of game, and the luxurious selfishness of the potentates of the establishment, how little genius is needed to make a nucleus for popular sympathy and indignation, out of a poacher and a dean! The extreme view of the social abuse each typifies, with a careful ignoring of their practical modification and complex relations, is all that is requisite. An American, habituated to the sight of prosperous labour, has only to see a spectral child emerge from the shaft of a coal mine, look at the pinched features of a female operative in one of the manufac-turing towns, or try to understand a barbarian Welsh peasant raving for work, in order to have his imagination excited to a degree of philanthropic intensity, adequate to the conception of a "moving tale."

The first walk I took on English ground, was upon Christmas Day, and in a quiet street, I was startled by a shout evidently from a host of children, but the pathos of the sound was inexpressible; it breathed a kind of smothered gladness; there was a latent despair in it strangely blent with infantile weakness. I inquired its meaning, and was answered: "It is the cheer of the workhouse children at the sight of meat." In the first coach-office I entered, two men, with lowering brows, were consulting about the pursuit of a fugitive, who had set fire to a hay-rick belonging to the vicar, in revenge for having paid away his last shilling for parish rates. On landing, I encountered the anomaly of a Custom-house officer acting as sentinel, who not being able to read, could not recognise the permit I offered for transferring baggage to the shore; and this was not an isolated fact, but a significant proof of the want of popular education in Great Britain.

The slow perception of the common people, and their utter want of interest in anything beyond their vocation, is one of the most striking contrasts to an American. Thousands are fated to a hopeless routine, from which there is no escape, nor any advancement in prospect for their children, except through emigration; stultified with beer and tobacco, it is difficult to obtain an intelligent response from any of the lower orders, to the most ordinary question. One sees in their stolid looks and incurious minds a fatal hopelessness, the natural consequence of a fixed and limited destiny; and taking the press as a chart whereby the degree and quality of national culture may be estimated, do we not daily find in the ferocious personalities and ungenerous comments on other governments, and in the revolting details of crime, painful traces of barbaric tastes? From the iron rule of a mercantile company in London over millions of Hindus, on the other side of the globe, to the savage delight exhibited by the mob in the bloody scenes of the ring, there is evident a gross love of brute force inconsistent with high civilization. The state trials of Great Britain involve tragedies deeper and more appalling than her literature embalms. A history of taxation in the kingdom would prove the keenest satire on its civilization. The most effective characters for pathetic novels to be found, are discoverable among the ushers and governesses of England. Lambeth Palace is a monument of ecclesiastical persecution. The most touching imaginable evidence of woman's appreciation of rare sympathy, is to be recognised in the small and united contributions of London sempstresses to Hood's monument. The most revolting instance of vulgar cupidity anywhere visible, occurs daily in the wretched little cabins of the English steamers that cross the Channel, where two burly sailors go round soliciting a gratuity from passengers prostrated by seasickness. A fat church dignitary, his skin rubicund with years of vinous circulation, reading a moiety of the service, which is completed by a poor, laborious canon, is the greatest conceivable satire upon Christianity. The hollow cough from unventilated rooms in smoky Staffordshire, pleads to the humane with keener emphasis, as the baying of the hounds vibrates over the green fields adjacent, proclaiming that a score of surfeited squires are enjoying the pure air after a sumptuous breakfast. In these, and a hundred other incidental experiences of the traveller in Great Britain, there are revelations of immense injustice to humanity; but the rational mind is ever aware that the possible evils of all systems are alleviated by individual conscience, good sense, and kindness; and that it would be as unphilosophical as unchristian to accept the exaggerated pictures of social abuses drawn by fanatical invention, as expositions of national character only those whose nature's plague it is "to pry into abuses," or those who studiously magnify the blots on the escutcheon of a people, can find delight in such a perversion of melancholy truth.

Although several weeks had elapsed since the Duke of Wellington's funeral, that event was still the prevalent idea. It seemed as if the demise of the most permanent and legitimate lion ever known to the metropolis, was destined only to prolong his reign. Besides the fixed memorials in the nation's heart, the statues and the princely abode, at every window was visible his "counterfeit presentment," in all the phases of his existence: at church, before the troops, in a morning walk, writing, reading, praying, asleep, and on horseback; in his castle, and his apartment at the Horse Guards, at club and church, and, finally, on his couch of death, as he lay in state. In the latter representation at Madame Tussaud's, the illusion was so complete as

to be shocking; it was difficult to realize that the livid wax was not the honoured chieftain's clay. To the citizens so long habituated to regard the Duke as the greatest man in England, perhaps there was nothing incongruous in the popular oblation to his memory; but to the stranger in London, in whose imagination he is an historical and not a local character, the attempt to draw the line between the sublime and the ridiculous, between familiar notoriety and universal respect, in these demonstrations, was by no means easy. In spite of the wish "to do him reverence," the question would suggest itself — what substitute for his nose can "Punch" discover?

When I saw the misty banners hanging about the chalky promontory of Dover, as the wind lashed the channel into foam, I thought of the hoary warden as a noble epitome of English honour and courage; the space he filled in the public eye seemed proportioned to the extent of his services, and the dignity of his office and name; and I felt a thrill at the grandeur of the vigil he seemed yet to keep on the natural ramparts of the sea-girt isle; but these associations were sadly invaded by the transition from hero-worship to cockneyism, from the idea of the conqueror at Waterloo to that of the lion of London.

The truth is that noble enthusiasm has no greater foe than the snob. Sycophancy trenches sadly upon the function of reverence. The defence to mere rank and title accuses the integrity of the tribute offered to genius and work. A party of English and Americans arrived together at the bridge of Menai, and their respective behaviour was characteristic; the Americans puzzled the guide with inquiries as to the mechanism and philosophy of the wonderful structure, while the first question of the English party was, "Where did Her Majesty stand?" A manly-looking yeoman we encountered at Chatsworth, was so eager to show us what we imagined would prove a novel specimen of the vegetable world, that we turned aside and followed a devious path, only to be amused at the look of solemn admiration with which he pointed to a couple of saplings, and informed us they were planted by the Queen and Prince Albert. It is this subserviency to artificial distinction which vulgarizes even true fame.

When I had satisfied the ardent curiosity, which for the first hour of my visit to Apsley House, riveted attention to the specimens of modern art which decorated its walls, and my mind was free to revert to those associations which identify it, as a whole, with the career of the great English soldier, I found that the Duke's simple and unadorned chamber most perfectly realized the idea of the chieftain as he lives in the imagination. The absence of ornament, the camp-bed, and meagre furniture, were in harmony with that self-denial and independence of the conventional, worthy of a hero.

That the residence of a wealthy English gentleman should be crowded with the best productions of artists, was a fact merely indicative of good taste and prosperity not unpleasing to contemplate. It was gratifying to the heart and conscience to think of a just reward for years of self-sacrifice and fidelity thus achieved. No more appropriate temple to enshrine the works of Landseer and Wilkie, the portraits of the brave and the gifted, and the luxurious appendages of domestic enjoyment, can be imagined, than the house of a devoted public servant and victorious officer. But the same feeling was not excited by a view of the trophies and emblems of his success. It seemed at once contrary to good taste, and discordant with the magnanimous spirit of true greatness, to place at the foot of the staircase, like a captive bound for ever to the wheels of his triumphant chariot, the colossal image of Napoleon, and to spread before his eyes the picture of his own successful battle-field. These may well be garnered, with the banners and regalia of the conquered foe, in the national halls, but to make them the familiar adornments of the soldier's house appeared rather the dictate of self-complacency than self-respect.

When I surveyed this apotheosis of self-esteem, while the Cockneys were absorbed in criticising Grant's "Melton Hunt," or looking through their eye-glasses, with many a chuckle, upon the marble brow of the devastating genius whose power was crushed under the supervision of their victorious Duke, I recognized in his abode the epitome and idea of an Englishman. The paramount good sense, the stern loyalty, the thorough conservatism, the systematic habits, vital integrity, practical but calm zeal, and native moderation of the Duke, were a sublimation and concentration of those qualities which ensure the material well-being and the respectability of the nation. There was more pride, however, than poetry in the scene, more of the prestige of success than the romance of genius; and it was difficult for the mind of the spectator to combine, in one person, the indefatigable young soldier of the East, the man who stemmed the torrent of war in the Peninsula, and who stood firm, patient, judicious, and resolved at Waterloo, with the venerable object of daily observation and record for such a long series of years in London. It was still the lion *versus* the hero.

CHAPTER VI

A DAY IN OXFORD

Oxford, ancient mother! hoary with ancestral honours, and haply, it may be, time-shattered power.

DE QUINCEY

It was New-Year's morning when I awoke in Oxford, but the anniversary so hilarious in my native land, there had what Byron calls an "old feel." The fashion of the upholstery seen from the canopied observatory of the stately bed, the profound stillness, a certain musty odour peculiar to venerable chambers, and the very design of the grate in which the remains of a huge coal-fire smouldered, betokened a conservative locality. A glance from the window confirmed the impression. The plaster had fallen, in many places, from the front of the opposite house, and the grey slates on the quaint gable-roofs were broken; the shops of stationer, tobacconist, and chemist displayed their wares meagrely, as if too well known to require advertisement; and near by rose the wide court walls, grey pillars, statues, and cornices of Queen's College. A gownsman, with square, silk cap, passed rapidly in the twilight of that winter morning; and, beyond the long range of buildings, masses of glazed twigs were printed on the leaden sky. Nor was the sensation of age lessened, when I descended the dark staircase to the large, dim coffee-room, with its tall columns and shadowy paintings. The waters moved slower, and were more deferential than elsewhere; their years, too accorded with the place; all was "grand, gloomy, and peculiar;" and, as I sat at my lonely breakfast in an angle of the spacious room, it seemed as if many a scholastic reverie and dream of literary fame, born of solitary enthusiasm, yet lingered in the silent air; and when, at evening, the white-haired host and hostess of "The Angel" bowed us out to the very coach-door, the day's experience closed with the sanction of an old and almost obsolete custom.

Each of the twenty-four Colleges has an individual charm, such as habit would naturally endear; and this accounts for the strong local attachment they inspire. In one a beautiful walk, in another the Gothic splendour of the chapel; here an organ of thrilling harmony, and there a hall with some favourite portrait; the mellow hues of a painted window, the exquisite workmanship of a shrine, and even, to epicurean imaginations, the delectable association of the refectory, are spells to win and hold the sympathies; a library, a choir, or a tree, such as here exist, may easily become the nucleus of youthful sentiment. In truth, Oxford typifies the luxury of knowledge; it is the scholar's paradise.

To the visitor from the New World, where our acquisitions are no sooner made than used, where we study to teach, and the active employment of learning is the very condition of its attainment, these ancient receptacles of science and letters, crowned with the graces of art, embosomed in the charms of nature, and hallowed by the memories of so many sages and bards, strike the imagination like an Eastern romance. To sleep in these dormitories, wander under these noble trees, pray in these beautiful chapels, explore unmolested and at leisure, for years, these records of the mind in all tongues, and of all ages, is to actualize a grand intellectual dream, and to grow calm in an atmosphere of wisdom. The noiseless doors, carpeted galleries, towers fretted by time, and made aerial in moonlight, features of the great departed beaming from the silent walls, green arcades to wander through in June, and dark-veined festal boards around which to cluster on winter nights, forms of saints and martyrs, tomes in which are garnered the choicest pearls of knowledge, hushed rooms opening on corridors dim with time, and vast quadrangles through which the spring bird's trill wakes the echoes of ages, form an environment to a contemplative nature, which unites the tranquillity of seclusion to the delights of taste.

It is not surprising that, to minds thus cradled, in their most susceptible era, the mere names of Oriel, All Souls', or Christ's, should become watchwords, in after-life, of endearment and inspiration. The poetry of academic life is here concentrated; study is idealized and consecrated, and the scholar's life enshrined. I roamed through the churches, halls, museums, and libraries of Oxford, with a new consciousness of the dignity of human nature. The old cassia-tree by the President's door at Magdalen, planted on the day of his inauguration sixty-five years ago, symbolized, in the slow gradations of its vegetable life, the mechanical existence of the unenlightened and unprogressive intellect, compared with the life here realized. I seemed to behold anew "the countenance of Truth in the still air of delightful studies."

Even a stranger recognises these distinctive features with a special interest; and they serve to impress each college on the memory. Thus the grooves and ivy-clad arches of Magdalen, the high trees of Christ's, the statue in the court of Brazenose, the sun-dial designed by Wren in the quadrangle of All Souls', individualize them in the retrospect. It was in the hollow square, enclosed by Queen's, that Webster made an agricultural speech, the eloquence of which is still lauded by the old porter; its library is exquisitely ornamented with Gibbons' carving. In the park of New College are yet traceable the fortifications of Cromwell's time. There is an oaken door in St. Mary's Church which once communicated with the Bocardo Prison, where Cranmer was in durance. Were it not for these and similar tokens, the visitor would retain but a confused idea of humid cloisters, dark chapels, pale escutcheons, inscribed entablatures, mellow pictures, and long ranges of crowded book-shelves.

The most characteristic and delightful indication of the different colleges, however, is to be found in the memorials of founders, benefactors, and graduates. One is hallowed by the grave but affable countenance of Jeremy Taylor, another by the monument to old Burton; here, as in life, may be seen the face of the author of the "Night Thoughts," and there that of the poet whose "Missionary Hymn" keeps his sacred zeal fresh in our thoughts. For the lawyer, there is the statue of Blackstone; for the painter, "Mary and Jesus after the Resurrection," by Mengs; for the geologist, crystal from Madagascar; now we are arrested by an altar-piece sculptured by Westmacott, and anon charmed with the glow of a Nativity window designed by

Reynolds. The corridor reminds us of the Camp Santo of Pisa in its silent and arched solitude; and an elm avenue with deer is like Chatsworth or Windsor; the black and moss-grown architecture of one nook is contrasted with the fresh wood and airy style of a modernized angle; one moment we enter an alcove, where a loving reader would be oblivious of time for hours, and the next behold an effigy whose grim quaintness transports us to the infancy of art; now we see an arrangement of candles and reading-desk in the chapel, so like Mother Church as at once to announce the head-quarters of Puseyism; and again look round the dining-room of the Fellows, upon the old silver, the easy-chairs, thick carpet, and dark mahogany, that invariably prophesy fine sirloins and old wine. Indeed, a most savoury odour from antique butteries often testified, during the survey, to that union of good viands and monastic shelter which song and legend attribute to the jolly friars.

The bowers of wisdom are not exempt from human weakness, and rank asserts its privileges here with the same emphasis as in the great world. Not only are there grades of scholastic title from servitor to dean, but there are those who drink beer and those whose beverage is port and sherry; there are dark, angular caps for the student, and a gay sash for the doctor of music; the greetings of the menial are graduated in the shades of the academy as in the halls of fashion, by these badges of distinction; the chancellor, regent, proctor, and steward, may bandy the "insolence of office;" the oldest Fellow awaits impatiently the death of him he trusts to succeed in dignity and emolument; the young aristocrat lords it over the yeoman's son, although such was the lineage of the martyr who here lighted up a fire "that has never gone out." Men of rare endowments indolently waste their energies in these pleasant halls, following out some idiosyncracy of their own, utterly valueless in its results; and men of vast erudition rust away that honour which a useful life can alone keep bright. The days of the isolated and monastic scholar have passed; a railway connects the University and the metropolis; public sentiment, national enterprise, and the spirit of the age, invade the retreats of learning, and demand, with a voice whose mandate cannot be neglected with impunity, that the scholar would now act with and serve his race.

In these cloistral and umbrageous haunts, how many of our favourite authors passed their youth! By this gate of Pembroke, Johnson improvised daily to a group of his fellow-students; somewhat of Addison's classic dignity was imbibed from the antique grandeur and verdant beauty of Magdalen, where he dwelt; and the walk that bears his name must have yielded him many a graceful image; for, as I followed its paths, even at that inclement season, the meadow it encloses was green, the elms and beeches hung their fantastic tracery in picturesque confusion overhead, and the notes of thrushes and robins rose cheerily from the hedge. The omniferous bibliopole, De Quincey, here laid up stores of reflective wisdom, afterwards bountifully dispensed through "The London Magazine;" and Chaucer here found the divining-rod that opened the "fount of English undefiled." No American can pass Berkeley's monument, in Christ's Church, without being gratefully minded of his bequest to the poor college of New England; or remember without emotion that here Roger Williams was educated. Jeffrey, the Edinburgh critic, here passed "a few uncomfortable years;" Sir Thomas More, Sir Walter Raleigh, Chillingsworth, Clarendon, Locke, Gibbon, and Fox, here studied.

Is it not a suggestive practical comment on university life, that the only names with which an ancient seat of learning is associated are those of a few authors? It is the light which radiates, not that which is enclosed, that vindicates scholarship. It is those men who, by the force of circumstances or the impulse of genius, dispensed the knowledge here acquired, that makes Oxford precious to the world. There is an intellectual aristocracy as selfishly exclusive as any based on wealth or title. "Small have continual plodders ever won," says Shakspere, "save base authority from others' books." The conservatism of learning is often as great an obstacle to humanity as that of ignorance. Oxford itself presents the anomaly of a monument to designate the spot where three of the most pious and brave of English churchmen were burned at the stake for anti-Catholic opinions — the progressors and students cheering with fiendish joy; and this in the very centre of national enlightenment. In our own time, a most pure, lofty, and disinterested youth of genius was ignominiously cast from her bosom; and Shelley, the he most needed the light of wisdom and the shelter of charity.

The system of buying themselves out of the prescribed routine, is an abuse which reduces the privileges of Oxford students to a merely technical form. tutorships and lectures, nay, books and cabinets, are obviously but so many external resources, the use and abuse of which are entirely dependent on the will of the recipient; and such is the perversity of human nature and the caprice of fortune, that intellectual achievement is often in the inverse ratio of outward advantage. Experience of life and means only realized through great exertion and sacrifice, have been and are the most efficient sources of mental growth; properly speaking, all men that are really educated, are self-educated; and it is the judgement, the labour, and the love of the scholar alone, that enable him, from the most complete armament, to gain, temper, and skilfully use, the weapons of learning.

It has been said that we are to the modern English author a kind of living posterity; and it may, with equal truth, be declared that the old authors of England are our intellectual ancestry; and I know not of a more interesting experience to the American traveller, than his first acquaintance with the authentic portraits of those whom he has long regarded as intimate literary benefactors. This enjoyment is realized in perfection in the picture-gallery of the Bodleian Library at Oxford. Guy Fawkes' lantern, and the letter that betrayed him; the theatre where the allied sovereigns received degrees after the battle of Waterloo; the antique orrery, the twisted arch, Cardinal Wolsey's chair, the carved roof, a large bell, and Dr. Pusey's lodgings, awaken and gratify his curiosity: but the lineaments of those he delights to honour, and whose productions have contributed to his own development, attract a higher sympathetic regard. Ranged as they are beside historical characters, the imagination is kept on the wings, as it expatiates in the different eras of English history, and revives the memories of genius that illustrated, adorned, or was sacrificed to them. To wander, for hours, through this silent multitude, comparing the expression of each with our previous conception, and with their characters as revealed in their books, is one of the most absorbing and delightful of the pleasures of Oxford.

There is Shirley, the dramatist, whose *penseroso* look accords entirely with the melancholy passion to which he gave such vivid utterance; Dryden, by Kneller, shows keen intelligence in his eye, which is full as the organ of language; at a later period his likeness gains in dignity by the altitude of the brow; his mouth, in both pictures, indicates a sensuous aptitude and a flexible will. Clarendon is the prototype of talent, superciliousness, and luxury. Sir Godfrey understood Addison perfectly: how coldly elegant and refined is his whole air; there is no ardour but much clearness in the eye; the cut of the lips is decidedly handsome, and the coat and wig are those of a gentleman. Compare him with Swift, who hangs near by: what a fiery eye, combative, wilful, arrogant, quick-tempered, and yet latently-genial look — too belligerent and egotistic, however, for the gown and bands. In striking contrast is the kindly, timid, and yet tasteful physiognomy of Prior. Now comes another of Vandyke's, Charles I; and the more we study the familiar countenance, the more inclined we shall be to agree with the superstitious Italian, who read therein a tragic fate. The corkscrew ringlets of Henrietta, and her blonde cheeks, suggest, however, no fit companion for such a destiny. Charles II, by Lely, adjacent, has a debauched air and a scornful play of features; his manners must have been indeed attractive, to neutralize the repulsive mould of the lower part of his fae. How fat and coarse appears Queen Anne, by Kneller, beside the pale, ruffed, and hooded Mary of Scotland, with her delicately chiselled features. James II looks exactly as conceited, narrow, and amorous, as history paints him. Duns Scotus has the aspect of an intellectual gladiator. Paracelsus, with his aquiline nose and muscular neck, his refined mouth and large cranium, unites the signs of mental vigour and acuteness. How keen is Locke's thin face; and how quaint Lord Burleigh going to Parliament on his mule. The next picture is a curiosity as well as a memorial; it is a "poker-drawing" — the head of Sir Philip Sydney burnt into wood by Dr. Griffith. The forehead is beautiful, the temples ideal, and the hair full of grace, with unusual space between the eyes. What a strong, clear, out-looking expression has Luther, as depicted by Holbein; a kind of bulldog tenacity joined to a tempered sweetness and frank courage — the whole Teutonic. Handel's brow is fine, but the upper lip is too long, and the expression is that of self-esteem. Scaliger's head is wonderful, a noble forehead over a mean lower face. Lord Stafford, as painted by Vandyke, while full of intelligence, has a vindictive look that baffles confidence. Sir Kenelm Digby is very handsome and expressive, the mouth loving, the eye wise, the beard picturesque, the chiaroscuro finely managed, and the whole effect generous and noble. Bishop Sprat's portrait incarnates clerical prosperity; there is something very sweet in Sir Thomas Browne's mouth, while his knowing eye, high and fair brow, dark moustache and wig, fresh complexion, and long visage, are quite worthy of a benign philosopher; his expression, when attentively sought, is that of subdued eagerness. Under him is Montaigne, with a full brow, a reddish moustache, and good nose; he wears a peaked beard and a sparse collar; the lips are full, especially the lower; it is a face of decided character, in which the prevailing expression is contemplative, more abstracted than observant. Dr. South has a vigorous look, accordant with his tone of mind; the lower jaw is of a sensuous mould, the eye is dreamy; and, altogether, there is something very fresh, strong, and acute, in the union of ruddy cheeks and dark visionary eyes, while a sardonic gleam modifies their expression. Butler looks sneering; Pope bright and handsome; Cowley old and discontented; Ben Johnson hale and bluff; Lord Eldon bullyish; and a portrait of Dr. Aldrich, by Reynolds, with open shirt-collar and fur-cap, is singularly lifelike. As I recognised the hard and firm purpose and the wily insight of Wolsey in Holbein's picture, I could not but compare it with Shakspere's:

"Though from an humble stock, undoubtedly
Was fashioned to much honour. From his cradle
He was a scholar, and a ripe and good one;
Exceeding wise, fair spoken, and persuading;
Lofty and sour to them who loved him not;
But to those men that sought him sweet as summer."

Dr. Clarke's face is fine; that of Grotius angular, with a square and by no means lofty forehead; Erasmus looks study-worn and misanthropic; Marlborough, in his bust, full of confidence, and the effect of his brilliant air is diminished by an arrogant expression.

The combination of town, rural attraction, and venerable

university buildings, enhances the effect of Oxford, when viewed from the roof of the Ratcliffe Library, or beheld in detail while passing through the streets. The towers rise at intervals from the midst of houses like hoary sentinels — the intellectual beacons of a kingdom whose prevailing features are material prosperity and need. Thick and lofty masses of foliage give a refreshing tone to the otherwise neutral hues of the picture. The meadows, so broad and green, through which flows the Isis, and the long vistas of leafy walks and shadowy turf, are the more pleasing, encountered, as they are, in the immediate vicinity of busy streets. The twilight of courts, halls, and chapels, is more impressive to the eye dazzled with the glare and variegated tints of shop-windows; and the meditative air of the galleries and chapter-house becomes thrice pleasing becaue the sights and sounds of ordinary life are audible without their quiet precincts. It is a great impulse to high association, to look up from one's daily meals to the noble array of renowned characters, whose early studies are identified with this asylum of knowledge. The celebrated Morales, representing Christ bearing His Cross; the magnificent antique head of Alexander, with lips parted in expressive power; the stained glass window — trophy of an obsolete art; and the picturesque sylvan glories of the place, unite in an harmonious inspiration in the ideal mood that so many relics excite. The sentiment of reverence hallows thus perpetually the scene of education, and gives an habitual sense of dignity to the pursuits which here engage the mind. Incalculable is the advantage thus gained to character.

No one, however, with the least moral sensibility, contemplates the rich variety of means, examples, and illustrations of human culture, thus garnered and centralized, without a painful consciousness of the inadequacy of his own singleness of aim and opportunities for intellectual development. So vast a field of inquiry, such an ample page of science, is revealed, even by a casual view, that we are oppressed at the wealth of ideas placed within the mental grasp, and humiliated at our own limited capacity. On the other hand, we recognize, with fresh perception, that law by which the mind can only assimilate what is kindred to itself; we remember that to each soul is given special endowments; that, to a great extent, the mathematician, the philologist, and the reasoner, are born such as truly as the poet;

and that only by strictly following the native tendency of his own instinctive gift, can the individual essentially improve. The difference between a Parr and a Bacon is felt at Oxford, where the annals of the University so clearly indicate the immense disparity between mere acquisition and original thought; the ability to furnish the mind, and to exercise it; the genius and the will to discover and promulgate new truth, and the ignoble narrowness that reposes, without an aspiration, within the formal entrenchments of the past.

CHAPTER VII

ART

In the Fine Arts mere imitation is fruitless; what we borrow from others must be again, as it were, born in us, to produce a poetical effect.

SCHLEGEL.

Comfort and utility are too exclusively the national ideal, for Art to be other than an exotic plant in England; where it is an indigenous product, the result, though often exquisite, is limited. A few deservedly celebrated native artists illustrate this department of human culture; but they are comparatively isolated. In no broad sense can Art be said to have attained the dignity of a national language, an expression and representation of the universal mind, as in ancient Greece, modern Italy, and Germany. The sense of beauty and devotion to the ideal are rare exceptions, not normal phases of English character. As a general truth, it may be declared that Art flourishes in Great Britain socially as an aristocratic element; popularly, under a humourous guise; and professionally, in the lives of a small number of men of decided genius. The absence of taste is manifest, at once, in the dwellings, the costume, and the ordinary arrangements of life; and when a shape or scene arrests the eye by its artistic merit, they are usually related to convenience and economy. In the landscape gardening, railway depôts, cutlery, fire-places, bridges, pottery, and hayricks, we often see the most striking grace, appropriateness, and skill; but seldom do the same characteristics assert themselves in domestic architecture or statuary. A tunnel, brewery, or chintz pattern are more significant of the national mind than exclusive forms of art. Beauty is chiefly allied to the service of trade and wealth. In vehicles and ship-building the Americans excel their brother utilitarians. As a use, Art is prolific in England, as an aspiration, sterile. The superb private collections are made up almost entirely of foreign pictures; and these, from the fact of their being an individual luxury, instead of a popular blessing, as on the continent, testify, like the conservatories filled with tropical flowers, to a rare and costly gratification. Look at the history of national development in literature, and on the stage, and how exuberant is the product, and general the appreciation, compared with that which attends the Fine Arts.

We have been reproached with our absurd imitation of classic models in public buildings, designed for purposes of mere convenience or traffic; but there are more anomalies in stone in London than of wood in the cities of America; no specimens of incongruous architecture can outvie many of the churches of the British metropolis. Club-houses boast there the most expensive embellishment; Cruikshank is the most popular limner; the engraver often grows rich, while the historical painter is driven to suicidal despair. And, in the case of successful men of genius, in the higher branches of Art, what is the process of their triumph over financial difficulties? that of noble patronage of academic favour. The most lucrative sphere of painting in England is portraiture; and to render it such, great ability must coincide with the endorsement of a clique, and the prestige of fashion. Reynolds and Lawrence were the oracles of the Royal Academy, and the pets of the aristocracy. Flaxman, Barry, and Gainsborough, were unappreciated while they lived. St. Paul's and Westminster Abbey are grand and memorable exceptions to the general dearth of architectural grandeur in a city of unequalled magnitude.

There are, too, special causes which limit the enjoyment of such Art as does exist. To view pictures is a contemplative act, one which demands time and self-possession; and he who has once acquired the habit of musing, by the hour, in the tribune of the Florence Gallery, or passing days in the halls of the Vatican, will scarcely endure twice the martyrdom of being led around by a gabbling *cicerone,* with a flock of other victims, to catch glimpses of the pictures in an English mansion. The very aspect of resorts intended to gratify taste, shows, to the practised eye, that Art is not native here, nor "to the manner born." Compare a London arcade with the Palais Royal, the arrangement of goods in a shop in Regent Street, and the manners of the attendant, with those encountered in the Rue Vivienne, or the Piazza San Marco; or a visit to the National Academy and the Louvre; how mean the surroundings, and commonplace the rooms of the one, and what magnificent saloons, and admirable order enchant you in the other. In Paris and Rome we seem to inhale an atmosphere of Art; it is a portion of existence, a familiar necessity; in London it must be painfully sought, and when found, often affects us like the sight of an eastern prince, with silken robe and pearly coronet, dragged along in a triumphal procession of northern invaders.

The acquisition of the Cartoons of Raphael, and the Elgin marbles, is no more an evidence of national Art, than the temporary deposit of the spoils of the Vatican in the Louvre. The best decorative Art in the kingdom is of foreign origin; Verrio was born in Naples, Gibbons in Holland. It is to the achievements and dominant taste of a country that we must look for proofs of her artistic genius; and it is remarkable what a large number of painters in England have excelled in special qualities, and risen to a certain point, without ever attaining the completeness of power, and fertility of result, which distinguish the Italian, Spanish, and Flemish masters. In the portraits of Jackson, Ramsey, Hoppner, Owen, Copley, Harlow, Opie, and others, there are distinctive excellences, but, in few instances are they unaccompanied by serious defects; and all these painters are so inferior to Vandyke and Titian, as to have failed in establishing a world-renowned school of portraiture. In Allan, Romney, Northcote, Mortimer, Burnet, Raeburn, and others, who tried their skill in a broader sphere, it is not acknowledged that the executive faculty was too limited and unreliable, to do justice to their respective genius? The vague and sublime effects of Martin are among the few specimens of modern English Art, that seem born of original inspiration. Haydon succeeded only in two or three instances, after countless experiments, as a disciple of high Art.

Indeed, it would seem, that the less ambitious the more successful, is the rule of Art in England, as evinced in the depth of tone and aerial distances of the water-colour painters, in such humble subjects as the "Corn-Field," and "Old Mill," of

Constable, and the sweet pastoral views of Wilson and Collins. In miniature, also, there are unrivalled painters; and innumerable amateurs, like Sir George Beaumont, who manifest the practical fruit of cultivated artistic taste, Etty's flesh-tints, Cooper's kine, and Cattermole's water-coloured pieces that bring six hundred guineas, are significant achievements of the English school.

The memorable phase of Art in England is her Gothic architecture; and the cathedral towns, by the spell of their solemnly beautiful and ancient temples, and the holy charm of their old church music, exalt the imagination and awe the heart; but the minister is the sublime trophy of primitive religious zeal, and the wealth of a splendid hierarchy; it sprang, like painting in Italy and Spain, from the inspiration of faith sustained by regal power; and cannot be deemed an exponent of the present national life or an evidence of existent artistic culture. A palace of crystal filled with the products of all nations, far better typifies the spirit of the age; temples erected to the genius of locomotion, framed of iron and roofed with glass, a choice specimen of Wedgewood ware, a highly-finished and expressive cabinet-picture, or an elaborate and graceful portrait, that shows high lineage in its whole air, and wealth in the costume and frame, are far more emblematic of the modern Art of the kingdom; and these, however excellent, have a limited and individual scope, at once indicative of utility and individual taste, rather than of grand national tendencies in the direction of independent Art. The best features of the latter, as manifested in the present century, is its commemorative design. However insensible to the beautiful, England never fails to obey the dictate of pride.

It is no less an instinct of national honour than of wise policy, to glorify in bronze and marble her heroes and men of science; and to a lover of his race, it is a high gratification to behold in St. Paul's the statues of Watt, Dr. Baillie, and Sir Astley Cooper, side by side with the effigies of Nelson, Sir John Moore, and Cornwallis. But even in the monumental tributes to her great men, we often see the most striking want of artistic intelligence. No better site for an equestrian statue can be imagined than that of the triumphal arch of Wellington, but how spiritless and awkward is the horse, and how stiff the figure of

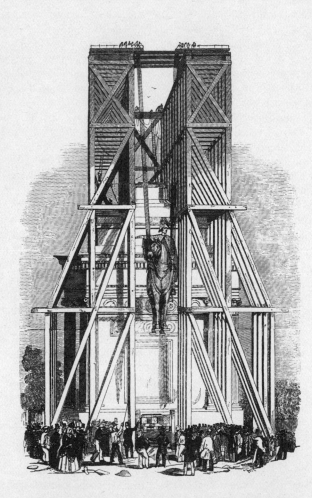

the Duke. What an absurdity to elaborate an allegory in marble, to illustrate the deeds of a naval hero, as is the case with the monument to Nelson in the Liverpool Exchange. Contrast Drury Lane with La Scala, one of Chantrey's funereal designs with Michael Angelo's Lorenzo or Canova's lions, and we see at once the instinctive impulse toward grandeur and comprehensive truth in the one case, and its comparative absence in the other.

The genius of Wren has chiefly redeemed London from the reproach of barbaric taste; Somerset House is palatial, and has a noble façade, and St. Paul's dome is pregnant with architectural sublimity; and yet how much the effect of these grand buildings is diminished by their position and crowded vicinage. Imagine the one with an open and ascending esplanade and background of verdure, such as environ the Pitti palace; and the other approached by a fine colonnade and broad square, with fountains such as front St. Peter's. The modified Gothic piles erected for the Houses of Parliament, as viewed from Lambeth Palace, certainly have an effective appearance; but the results aimed at, even at the enormous expense incurred, seem not to have been realized, either ideally, if we may trust the criticisms of artists, nor practically, if we justify the complaints of those for whose comfort and use the imposing structure was reared. In order to be recognised as characteristic of a nation, Art must prevail and declare itself in the general aspect and the minute detail of dwellings, streets, and households. We must behold it in the exquisite cornice, the noble portico, in the ornaments of the drawing-room, in the dress and equipage. When it is exhibited in a few memorable instances alone, their very singularity and perfection mark the absence of general taste; their merit, however transcendent, is exceptional.

It may be objected to the estimate of English Art by a traveller, whose time and opportunities are limited, that its main treasures are enshrined in private abodes, and only a superficial idea can be formed of them by the stranger. But this very seclusion accuses the prevalence and nationality of Art; it does not apply to Italy, France, and Germany, where he who runs may read the genius of the people in its artistic efflorescence. Average specimens also of each English master are to be seen in the galleries open to visitors; and the higher class of periodicals devoted to the subject, as well as many biographies and criticisms, have rendered its essential qualities familiar to every intelligent American.

The most impressive of his experiences in London, is when he reads Wren's epitaph in St. Paul's, and in obedience to its counsel, looks around and especially upward, to behold the great architect's monument. In original enterprise the water-colour exhibition will prove an agreeable surprise; the English have here achieved wonders. As an accomplishment, drawing is widely cultivated; and in almost every dwelling, from the middle class to the high nobility, a taste for Art is evident in some gem by an old master, the heir-loom of generations, or the recent and dearly-purchased acquisition from a modern pencil; and often in a most creditable specimen of domestic skill. These amenities have not lessened the coarseness of the lower orders. The rude fac-similes preserved by Mayhew, indicate that what he calls street-art, has not advanced since the Restoration. In London, an elegant edition of Sir Joshua's "Discourses" graces the nobleman's library; in Florence, the mutilation of a statue excites the common people almost to revolutionary frenzy; in the one place Art is thus a luxury of the educated, in the other a popular interest.

It is from the neighbouring scenery of Scotland and Wales, from the beautiful skies of Italy, and the poetic imagery of the East, that the English painter derives picturesque ideas. There are, indeed, craggy uplands, romantic lakes, and desolate moors, that afford impressive scenic materials, but the prevalence of level and highly-cultivated land, obliges the artist, who affects home subjects, to make up for the deficiency of grand features in the landscape, by a skilful use of the casual effects of nature, as in the living tints and almost moving clouds of Constable, and the breezy sea-coasts of Stanfield, and to resort to the minute language of common life, or its idealized personation.

It is a notable instance of the law of compensation, that the comparative absence of remarkable scenery in England, has thus given rise to the characteristic excellences of her school of painting, as the flatness of the Low Countries induced superiority of still-life in Flemish pictures. The vicissitudes of the climate, also, by concentrating enjoyment within doors, has led to a passion for collection and *vertu,* and thus indirectly promoted a taste for art. The literature of England is rich also in the eloquent exposition of the subject; and few works are so redolent of intelligent enthusiasm, in this regard, as those of Walpole, Reynolds, Beckford, Northcote, Hazlitt, Eastlake, Mrs. Jameson, Ruskin, and others.

There is far less taste for music, however, among the masses in England than those of America. "Chaque musicien," says a French writer, speaking of an English orchestra, "selon l'usage joua son air favori, avec cette noble indépendence qui caractérise l'artiste Anglais." A piano is to be found even in dwellings on the outskirts of civilization in this country; but some of the best English writers ridicule the Italian Opera; and a London audience, except when composed mainly of the aristocracy, prefer one of Dibdin's songs to the sweetest cavatinas of Bellini; their sympathies do not rise above the National Anthem. "All's Well" and the "Bay of Biscay" bring down the house, when "Vi ravisso" or "Non più mesta" would only provoke a yawn. The ballad to the common heart is more attractive than the lyrical drama. It is otherwise in Church music. Handel's popularity was remarkable, and, of elaborate composition, the oratorio is the favourite.

One of the most desirable of recent artistic institutions is the School of Practical Art, the rooms of which are above the Vernon Gallery. It is a palpable evidence of the consciousness of deficient national taste; and is intended as a corrective of the incongruous and ugly style of dress and furniture which deform the persons and homes of the English, specimens are here exhibited of good and bad patterns in articles of domestic economy, ornaments, and fabrics; and a catalogue *raisonné* explains the principle both of objection and preference; so that, even without any great sense of beauty, the visitor, when thus enlightened, may be horrified at the sight of his own pantaloons and drawing-room carpet, and take an initiative practical lesson in the appropriate, that may lead finally to the appreciation of high Art.

Nature herself has abridged the artistic development of England; her climate is unfavourable to ideal achievement, and to that elemental harmony between atmosphere, light, and temperature, and the purposes and effects of the artist, which render Italy and Greece a paradise in comparison. A dome or a column should point itself against a densely blue sky to be truly effective; a cadenza should ring through such a crystal air as hangs over Naples or Mexico, to reveal its sweetest melody; and colour, to be transparent and vivid, must be studied where the purple evening mantles with radiant hues the Adriatic Sea. Marble grows black and bronze corrodes in England, when exposed to air; how like a fossil coal looks Canning's form, and what a sooty hue invests Nelson, as the metal and the stone have become superficially decomposed by moisture. Half the time we must shiver instead of being cheered at the sight and sound of a fountain; and walking round St. Paul's, the walls look as if snow and soot had alternately drifted against them — especially the latter. The chiaroscuro made by smoke, gas, and drizzle, do not promote a desirable *relievo* in objects architectural or statuesque; the absence of the sun keeps invisible the more delicate touches of Leonardo and the finer tints of Claude on the noble's wall; and even the daguerreotypist must watch, like the fog-shrouded navigator on the Banks, for days before he can "get the sun." In such a climate great thinkers and indefatigable artizans prosper; but Art must be aided by pilgrimages to clearer horizons, and to latitudes where the firmament is oftener visible, and at home it will inevitably require the hot-bed of munificent patronage.

Of the national depositories of Art, there is none that charms the stranger like Hampton Court, and this primarily for other reasons than the ostensible one of its beautiful array of pictures. The rural attractions, the historical memories, and, not least, the weekly freedom of the palace and grounds, enjoyed by all classes and ranks, combine to make it one of the most delightful resorts in the vicinity of London. The moment you enter the old park, the stone archway, venerable trees, and groups of deer, attest the luxurious abode of the ambitious churchman, which, in a mood between fear and policy, he tendered as a gift to Henry VIII.

Even in winter, the bay, myrtles, and holly that line the smooth gravel-walks and level turf, give the approach to the vast old mansion a cheerful look; and when, as on the day of our visit, birds and sunshine enliven the place, it quite fulfils the idea of magnificence and scenic beauty attached to the reign of the uxorious and extravagant monarch whose ecclesiastical vice-regent adorned and enriched it. The old brick quadrangle, the mixed style of architecture, umbrageous alleys, terraced lawns, and dense clumps of shrubbery, unite to give an impression of grace, verdure, and antiquity, such as we derive from the Poggio Imperiale on the Villa Borghese; but the people who throng the grounds, and cluster round the flower-beds, are too northern in their physiognomies and costume to be mistaken for Romans or Tuscans: and it is delightful to witness the glow of pleasure on the honest face of some pallid artisan, and even the complacant strut of a bedizened London apprentice, as they taste the unwonted joy of a day of freedom amid the charms of Nature and the loveliness of Art.

Within, Hampton Court is a domain of picturesque history; and nowhere in the kingdom is Art more genially presented to the eye and mind: the ample light, the quiet, leafy garden visible through the capacious windows, the consciousness of a privilege to which all are admitted, and the liberty to roam, gaze and comment as we list, renders the scene, however familiar in some of its aspects, a memorable and grateful one to the traveller. Through the apparently endless succession of rooms he moves for hours, scarcely conscious of himself or of time, as he meets the eyes of men and women heretofore only known in histories, memoirs, plays, and novels. It is a kind of imaginative Court presentation, which infinitely excels in interest the actual ceremony; for it is not to strangers that he is introduced: he knows their origin, their triumphs, and their peccadilloes; but here, for the first time, their forms and faces are revealed.

In the midst of the pictured beauties of Charles II's Court, there is brought to a focus the spirit, the pageantry, and the tone of manners that mark the era of the Restoration. The dress, and the want of it, in this brilliant throng of fair and frail ladies; the very complacency of Nell Gwynne's lips; the contour, expression, and tints of the portraits, reflect more vividly than the historic page, the rebound from puritan rigour to the levity and abandon of a profligate Court. Sir Peter Lely becomes a more graphic chronicler than Grammont or Hume, for natural exceeds written language in moral significance. The sinister face of Buckingham, and the brazen charms of the Duchess of Portsmouth, more impressively than print, announce the lapse of England's civic glory. Many of the male portraits are familiar, not only from their constant repetition through the burin, but from the copies or duplicates to be seen in all the large English and many of the foreign collections — evidences of the efficient pencils of Holbein and Vandyke.

Interspersed with these, however, are numerous gems of Italian and Dutch Art, which rivet attention. I noted especially

Titian's "Uncle," and "Loyola" by the same artist; a "Virgin and Child," by Andrew del Sarto; the "Family of Pordenone," by himself; and a "Venetian Senator," also from his pencil; a "Knight of Malta," by Tintoretto; a "Magdalen's Head," by Sasso Ferrato; "Still-Life," by Kalf; a "Jewish Rabbi," and also a "Dutch Lady,' by Rembrandt and a "Magdalen," by young Palma. How suggestive to the fancy are admirably-executed portraits, with these generic and anonymous titles. Whole episodes of history and chapters of romance are mysteriously linked with the very names; anecdotes of the painters occur to the mind, and tragic legends, in which exactly such looking rabbis, knights, senators, and ladies have figured.

Undoubtedly a valuable lesson acquired at Hampton Court, is to appreciate the art and the science, too, of portrait-painting. In the hands of Vandyke and Titian, how it is sublimated into historical dignity; in those of Kneller and Lely, what an entire phase of fashion and meretricious female beauty it elaborates; with Reynolds, how much characterization it unfolds. To the American visitor the pictures of West here preserved have a special interest; they are monuments of industry, and, within certain limits, of genius, but the ability to create expression in this virtuous artist does not attain a standard to justify his more ambitious, and especially his religious limning.

It was before the old tapestry, and in the great hall of Hampton Court, that I chiefly reverted to its local associations; on the lawn, rural beauty keeps the eye, and in the presence-chambers and drawing-rooms, we are absorbed in the pictures; but under the Gothic carving of this roof, we recall the singular fact that the fall of Wolsey, as dramatized by Shakspere, was represented here upon the very scene where he ruled in splendour; and that Hampton Court itself, now, to the glory of civilization, made a shrine of Art to which the poor multitude may turn for refreshment, was, for centuries, the luxurious home of royalty, where the powerful of the realm resorted to celebrate a feast, hold an ecclesiastical counsel, or a chapter of the Order of the Garter, perform the nuptial ceremony, usher a royal scion into life, take refuge from pestilence, or enjoy a honeymoon.

I had anticipated no little pleasure from the English school of painting; to one acquainted with the galleries of Italy, but a

moiety of the collections of Dulwich and Blenheim have the attraction of novelty, and it is a delightful experiment for the American to verify, from actual inspection, his fragmentary knowledge of the artists who, during the present century, have given reputation to Great Britain as the nursery of an unique department of Art. The best public exhibition to gratify this natural desire, is the Vernon Gallery, so called from its chief benefactor, although many pictures are there to be seen which formerly adorned the walls of the National Gallery. At Marlborough House I enjoyed a first view of many originals, already established favourites through excellent engravings.

The epithet, clever, is often on the lips of Englishmen; it is a term which rightly designates the quality of their modern painting; truth to a special phase of nature, rare felicity of execution, wonderful tact and precision, and a genial development of character quite Shaksperian in its details, render these works at once peculiar and satisfactory; they charm without transporting, realize completely a limited ideal, and afford precisely such results as please, win, and enlighten, without awakening any profound emotion. They are usually gems rather than miracles of Art, perfect achievements within the bounds of natural observation, evidences of inimitable skill, but seldom of lofty inspiration. Here I recognized the dewy freshness, and almost sensible wind of Constable, the marvellous expression caught from real life by Wilkie, Etty's vivid colouring, the vital glow of Collins, the fine play-scenes of Maclise, and the significant compositions of Mulready.

It is a rare study of the elements of character, as revealed in faces and attitudes, to peruse intently the "Blind Fiddler" and "The Peep o' Day;" Lee's "Coast of Lincolnshire," Danby's "Fisherman's House," Calcott's "Returning from Market," and Gainsborough's "Drinking-Place," abound in local integrity of treatment. That graceful branch of the rainbow-art, which seems to reflect in colours the most refined episodes of the comic Muse, here displays its select triumphs in Newton's "Yorick and Grisette," and Leslie's "Sancho" and "Uncle Toby." For entire completeness of scope, a thorough success that baffles criticism, and, like Nature herself, simply demands recognition, Landseer's works seem to me unrivalled. If we apply to them Göthe's test, and judge each by its own law, however we may speculate about the rank of the branch of Art itself, there can be but one opinion of their intrinsic excellence. There are spaniels on his canvas here, that you long to pat, and expect to frisk, and the canine illustration of high and low life is so expressively true, that the genealogy of curs seems newly demonstrated, as an emphatic law of natural history.

The pictures of Landseer accuse our unappreciative observation most eloquently; animal life, its diversity of expression, its organized significance, and its subtle language, seems now made truly evident to the mind for the first time, and the senses attest its reality. From the breathing lions of Apsley House to the dead game at Chatsworth, from the fleeces of the sheep in

"Peace," to the head of the dying horse in "War," that excite our sympathetic admiration here, with what an exquisite refinement of perception, and miraculous touch of the pencil, is every hair made to glint, each nostril to dilate, and the eyes to gleam with ruminating pathos, or carnivorous zest. Landseer has idealized the animal sympathies of his countrymen; that instinct whose coarse manifestation appears in the zeal of the sportsman, in the relish of the beef-eater, in the sports of the ring and the cock-pit, refined to an artistic taste, gratifies the practised view of hunter and jockey, and, in a higher sense, the love of noble and graceful animals as objects of study and affection. But this painter has won a greater name than that of an inimitably skilful limner of animals; he has found the art of rendering them subsidiary to the grandest moral aim, as in the allegorical pictures we have named.

Another painter, who emphatically asserts the individuality of English Art, and whose best works give peculiar interest to this collection is Hogarth. Here again are we impressed with the intensity and special bounds of the national genius in this department. The irony of these creations, the palpable way in which human nature is exhibited in the most barren aspects of social life, the grim humour and bitter knowledge of the world visible in the "Marriage à la Mode," the "Dissipated Husband," the "Toilet of the Fine Lady," &c., while they gain instant applause for subtle characterization and leave a profound moral impression, are, at the same time, most skilful elaborations of the prosaic and conventional extremes of life. Hogarth's lessons are stern, his observation authentic, and his execution severely true; but these essential qualities of the artist are made to illustrate painful and artificial traits and local manners; we admire the consummate talent, while we grow sad before the misanthropic spirit of the artist. Probably no series of pictures are more widely or satisfactorily known, through engraved copies; still it is a great pleasure to examine the famous originals, and to behold, for ourselves, the actual source of those pictured moralities, and acts in the drama of modern life, which have never been artistically embodied by any other limner with like power.

Mulready, Webster, Redgrave, Ward, and Heming, excel in pictures of humble life, as the "Dame School," in satirical hits, and in the by-way comicalities of ordinary life. The whole range of artists thus endowed, may be considered as humorous; their *forte* is analogous to the sphere in literature made delightful by a class of writers scarcely known in any other country. The water views of Stanfield have singular merit. His harbours and lake scenes are wonderfully pellucid and picturesque; and whether it is the Zuyder Zee or Lake Como, there is a memorable freshness and vigour in his landscapes.

Several pictures of Turner's arrest the steps of the visitor, and win him to a mood of deeper attention as he glances with a smile of amusement, or a start of eagerness, from one to the other gem of this charming collection. These specimens of the great landscape artist, and those at the National Gallery, were to me the most interesting of all the pictures seen in England; my curiosity had been roused to the highest pitch by the brilliant rhetoric of Ruskin, and the apparently irreconcilable extremes of praise and censure of which Turner had so long been the subject; I found the enthusiasm of his eloquent admirer fully justified, and the diverse estimates of other critics satisfactorily explained. It is obvious, even from the few but characteristic pictures in the two galleries, that, like all men of original genius, Turner arrived at the most splendid triumphs through experiment. He seems to have thrown the whole force of artistic intelligence and manful endeavour into the world of light and colour, by living therein, sometimes extravagantly dallying with tints, at others seizing on the law of perspective, now patiently observant, and again boldly adventurous, until he wrested the secret and caught the manner of nature. Accordingly the word "daubs," like the blended patches on a smirched palate, do not unjustly describe some of his earlier pictures; while the highest eulogiums of his gifted advocate, inadequately represent the perfect and unequalled effects apparent in his subsequent and more felicitous works. Certain it is, that the "Misty Morning," and the "Ruins of Carthage," are the greatest conceivable triumphs in aerial perspective; architecture and atmosphere were never before made to figure on canvas as they do in nature, from the most grand to the most detailed truth of effect; before no other landscape is it possible so to launch the vision into the crystal vistas of tremulous mist and limitless horizons. The very idea of distance and imitation is lost in the consciousness of reality.

I imagine that the very defects of his own climate, as a school for colour, promoted this extraordinary success by the force of contrast; he seems actually to revel in the reproduction of the skies and atmosphere of the Orient and the South; his eye takes in with greater zest and precision, and his hand delineates with keener zeal, their clearness, brilliancy, and golden vapours, from the gusto born of deprivation. The Cuyps and Canalettos around, pale to a commonplace and partial truthfulness before these magnificent productions; but the Claudes ranged by their side, do not warrant the disparagement of Ruskin; making allowance for the inferior still-life and figures of Lorraine, and the effect of time in obscuring his tints, the sunsets of this exquisite artist glow also through a tremulous mist, and reveal a mellow depth, evidently derived from the same principle, and as much the result of genuine artistic inspiration as those of Turner. In his ardour for his idol, Ruskin occasionally becomes a special pleader, and is grossly unjust to the old masters.

The obscurity that shrouds the life of Turner and his eccentric habits, are well-known. That he was a barber's son, and changed his lodgings, and concealed his name, to enjoy the privacy so difficult for the man of acknowledged talent in England, are familiar anecdotes; but I was unaware of the extent to which his fame is, so to speak, impersonal, until I happened to be present when the publisher of the "Liber Fluvorum" received the messenger he had despatched to consult parish records and old acquaintances of Turner's, in order to learn some important dates to enter in the memoir attached to the new edition of the work; after the most patient investigation, it was found impossible to learn, with certainty, even the year of his birth.

A striking proof of the cleverness of the existent school of English painters, is manifest in the impromptu drawings of the Sketch Club. The members meet successively at each other's houses, once a month; a subject is given out, and precisely two hours occupied in its illustration. The theme of the sketches I examined was "Night;" and it was truly marvellous to witness, not only the completeness attained in so short a time, but the great variety of treatment. Stanfield had made a capital design for a landscape representing a midnight gale at sea; the drifting clouds, black waters, and heaving ship, were done to the life; another gave the moonlight scene from "The Merchant of Venice," with magical grace; and a third, whose turn was for comedy rather than sentiment, most graphically sketched the interior of a London court-yard, at midnight, with its deep shadows, adjacent roofs, and dark pavements, where two of the feline race, with upheaved backs, were caterwauling, to the immense discomfiture of an old gentleman, who looked down threateningly, in his night-cap, from a high window, while a couple of jovial strollers, primed for a lark, were quizzing him from below. A thorough mastery of detail in the use of the crayon. great knowledge of expression, as well as executive facility, were evident in all these impromptu drawings.

An American or Italian artist can scarcely realize the exclusive life of a skilful British painter of the present day. He works almost under the eye of his noble patron, with a quiet and gradual approximation toward the end they mutually seek. A picture is considered well before it is undertaken; the desire to please an individual gives unity of purpose, the certainty of adequate remuneration quells restless anxiety, and often a most intelligent sympathy and generous friendship encourages and cheers the artist. We have only to revert to the correspondence between Sir George Beaumont and Wilkie, to perceive the beauty and interest of the relation thus established between the man of genius and the liberal and tasteful man of wealth.

The system has its advantages and its objections; while the stimulus of personal motive is abundant, the existence and labour of the painter are often isolated; he is in danger of subserviency, and the guineas and seat at an aristocratic table, may trench upon that independence of mind so essential to great artistic achievement. Yet, as a general rule, the wise and discriminating as well as munificent patronage, under which the works of the English school have so often been created, is honourable, in the highest degree, to both artist and amateur.

The interest with which the pursuit of Art has always been invested, to my mind, became unusually vivid as I passed rapidly, one April-like morning, along the Edgware Road, towards the domicile of our countryman, Leslie, for whom I had been intrusted with a mission from one of his dearest relatives at home. As the cab rattled by many an old dwelling with ivy

twined about its base, and through lines of teams and butchers'
carts, I could not but acknowledge once more the force of that
instinct which, in the midst of so much bustle, and in the heart
of such material life, can bind a man to his easel, and
concentrate his mind upon the worship of beauty, while all
around him swells the vast tide of conventional affairs.

We drew up, at length, in the region called St. John's Wood,
before a modern house with a villa-like entrance, and, in a few
moments, I was cordially welcomed to the studio of Leslie. He
was engaged upon a picture that struck me as remarkably
adapted to his genius; the subject is the festive scene so minutely
described in the "Rape of the Lock." I wondered so fertile a
theme had never before seized upon the fancy of a painter, and
felt, as I gazed, that it was fortunately reserved for the graceful
delineator of "Slender and Anne Page," "Victoria's Coronation,"
and so many other gems of the same description. The consummate tact with which such an array of figures were grouped on
the canvas — all of cabinet size — the variety of expression and
costume, and the compact significance and authenticity of the
whole, not only as an illustration of Pope's conception, but of
the age it embodies, assured me that it would prove a felicitous
master-piece. I have never seen a picture of Leslie's so radiant
and, at the same time, well toned; as a study of colour, as well as
social life, it was exquisite; and the figure and face of Belinda
were all imagination could desire; not a trait was overlooked, not
a charm neglected; and I saw, with delight, that —

> "On her white breast a sparkling cross she wore,
> That Jews might kiss and infidels adore."

Leslie threw open the window just as a gleam of sunshine fell
on the distant hills, lightly veiled with pearly mist, over which it
is his custom to wander on summer mornings, and designated
the church-spire in whose shadow Constable is buried. The
landscape was thoroughly English. I had lately perused the
beautiful letters and not less beautiful life of Constable written
by Leslie, and now listened with peculiar satisfaction to his
glowing description and his tender regrets as he spoke of his
friend. No other painter so truly caught the vernal life and living
clouds such as, at this moment, expanded to our vision; and I
blessed the poetic justice which thus located his sepulchre amid

the scenes he loved to depict, and within the habitual ken of his brother-artist. I have often traced the analogy that exists between the individual phases of genius as exhibited in literature and art; and now again realized the intimate relation between the English humorists and such painters as Newton and Leslie; the sympathy the latter manifested in his inquiries about Irving confirmed the idea. Their artistic spheres are essentially alike; they both have charmed the world with the most genial and effective cabinet pictures, drawn from the more refined aspects of life, and finished to the highest point of grace and harmony.

CHAPTER VIII

CASTLES AND SHAKSPERE

This castle hath a pleasant seat; the air
Nimbly and sweetly recommends itself
Unto our gentle senses.

MACBETH

There, Shakspere! on whose forehead climb
The crowns o' the world! Oh, eyes sublime,
With tears and laughter for all time.

ELIZABETH BROWNING

The locomotive facilities of our day, if, on the one hand, they abridge poetic experience by rapidity and unadventurous order, on the other, enhance it by concentrating space and associations. Nowhere is this benefit more apparent than in England; and in no region of the kingdom has the traveller more reason to bless the miracles of modern conveyance, than where the iron network of the railway brings into such neighbourhood Stratford, Warwick, and Kenilworth. The local genius of each of these old towns is nearly related to the other, at least in the imagination; for they are alike hallowed by the spells of bard and baron: if in one we become absorbed in the feudal past, with all its valour, superstition, and intrigue, they most effectively reappear as described by the poet whose birth-place is adjacent; and if, in another, fancy delights to picture the early days of the minstrel, it is to link his mature triumphs with the historical relics and the natural beauty that make up the rest of the memorable picture. It is true that the details of chronology, and the heir-looms of power, at first, rivet attention in the castles; but, ere long, the portrait of an historical character, the trophy of a dramatic event, a glimpse of the Avon through an armorial window, or the sight of a sylvan patriarch asserting the departed glory of the forest of Arden, bring us again to the feet of Shakspere.

I have suggested that the most vivid impression of rural magnificance, as exhibited in the ancient domains of the

nobility, is obtained by viewing them when fresh from a manufacturing district; and this is the case because the luxury and the wretchedness thus contrasted are the result of modern times; high present cultivation in one case, and incessant labour in the other. But when we seek to become familiar with the baronial grandeur of England, to revive the epoch when earls confronted kings in battle-array, and the warlike and noble subject vied with royalty in the strength as well as the splendour of his abode, it is advisable to seek another contrast — that between the highly civilized life of to-day, as represented in a town built up by fashion and wealth, and the venerable castellated edifice that symbolizes the feudal and culminating era of British power. The elegant comfort and unfortified homes of our own times, their domestic privacy and gentle manners, are thus made to illustrate more picturesquely the massive towers, and huge grey battlements, wherein once the ambitious and titled of the land could only make sure their privileges.

The cawing of rooks from the inn-garden at Leamington, greets the ear of the awakening traveller as a sound consonant with ancient rural domesticity; and when he walks forth into the broad, cleanly-paved street, how fresh, eligible, and refined, is the aspect of all around, compared with the murky and toilsome look of a manufacturing town. Instead of a pale operative or surly carman, he encounters a well-varnished bath-chair, in which is seated an invalid dowager, with dark-silk pelisse, elaborate bonnet, and an air of dignified prosperity, drawn by a groom in livery; or he notes a gentleman in hunting-coat and gaiters, mounted on a sleek trotter; or he passes a handsome mansion, its front yard umbrageous with flowering shrubs, turns to mark the cheerful faces of two rosy young ladies in a snug pony-chaise, or enters a library on whose tables lie the journals of the day, the last novel, and the new poem, in convenient array. No sign of trade is visible, except in the attractive windows of a fancy-shop. The beautiful domicile of a renowned physician; an evergreen oak by the wayside, crowned with the traditions of ages; well-dressed people conversing at an angle, or taking their morning stroll, are the familiar objects; and the very breeze that plays over the scene has an unwonted freshness.

From this delightful sojourn — an epitome of English comfort in the nineteenth century — a visit to the neighbouring castle is like shifting the locality in a melodrama from the epoch of Victoria to that of Elizabeth. There are about the town of Warwick striking continental features, especially as it is revealed by the half-lateral rays of a declining sun. The range of flourishing vegetable-gardens that line the road by which it is approached, are, indeed, thoroughly English; but the heavy, antique gateway under which the coach soon rumbles, the stone buildings, and steep, rough thoroughfare, recall many a provincial city of southern Europe; and this idea is confirmed by the unexpected appearance of St. John's School, its large grey front, and avenue of tall pines, the mossy effigies of two goats rampant over the postern columns, its venerable and lonely court, and quaint windows. Before this olden spell is broken, a ramble to Guy's Cliff, while it elaborates the impression, links with it a cheerfulness such as Nature ever throws around the trophies of Art. The hedges of camelia and sweet-briar gladden the eye; the ancient box-trees, the weedy fountains, labyrinthine myrtle walks, and dripping grottoes, awaken vivid memories of the Boboli and Borghese Gardens; while the holly and ivy declare that the beautiful domain is in England.

It requires not Dugdale's testimony to convince us that this picturesque and verdant scene was, in remote ages, a place of religious seclusion; nor could imagination invent a more romantic hermitage for the adventurous and stalwart Guy to conclude devoutly his life of active heroism. If no monument, like that of Piers Gaveston, "the object of a monarch's love and victim of a subject's hate," was to be found, the spirit of romance, inevitably kindled by the cascades, rocks, glades, limitless meadow-sweeps, and distant, nestling churches, would conjure from tradition or fancy a tale of devotion and of sacrifice. The chapel, cave, and gigantic statue of the famous Earl, however effective in themselves, do not excite the mind to credulous aspiration like the view of the Cliff itself from the old mill — fit scene of the vigil and sepulchre of one of those heroes whose prowess and fortunes, equally chronicled by nursery legend and grave history, have just enough foundation in truth to justify the enthusiast at such a locality in yielding to a kind of visionary credence which boasts a charm to the poetic sense, it would be an ungracious task to destroy. His personal relics, exhibited by the ancient portress of the lodge at Warwick Castle, derive a new authenticity from the sentiment in regard to him we thus acquire at the Cliff. Her monotonous and pedantic recitative, as she wakes the echoes of the herculean porridge-pot, and displays the items of enormous armour, is listened to with less impatience, for the respect we have learned for Guy the Recluse enables us to accept, with diminished misgiving, the tangible proofs thus adduced of the capacity of his stomach and the power of his arm.

Once within the spacious court-yard, beneath those lofty towers and ivy-clad battlements, and in the shade of the glorious old oaks, firs, and cedars of Lebanon, the special memory of the wonderful Earl is lost in those broad associations which identify Warwick Castle with the prime of England's baronial history. Here the past of Britain is embodied. The massive and wonderfully-conserved structure was the home of the greatest subject of the realm. The concentrated relics of nine centuries are around us. We are in the midst of England, and also in the midst of her annals. This magnificent chestnut-tree, those shining arbutus-leaves, that wide-spreading and fresh-tinted vine-drapery, are triumphs of vegetable life which attest the vital phenomena of the hour; but the carved wainscot of the dead wood, against which hang the pictured faces of so many departed men and women, whose names are stamped on an immortal page, assure us, the instant we cross the threshold, that this living garniture decorates a mighty home of the past. Not in tedious genealogies, or barren royal successions, can we waste this hour of precious communion; as we look back and around, only what poetry has redeemed blends with the fair landscape and suggestive relics.

The proverb which declares an Englishman's home to be his castle, here gains an impressive significance. The road that conducts us from the lodge to the court, is excavated from a solid rock, and canopied with verdure; while the towering line of fortified wall, roof, and bulwark, convey at once a sense of the impregnable, the complete, and the time-hallowed. It needs not the absent portcullis and overgrown moat, nor the arch which now takes the place of the drawbridge, to indicate a haunt of power capable of the most prolonged defiance. Caesar's tower, alone, which dates from the Roman conquest, in its irregular outline and venerable strength, fills the imagination, like an invulnerable beacon on the shores of elder time, casting its shadow on the bright green turf, as when it fell on the grim old earls or knightly barons eight hundred years ago. The massive stonework, aged and lofty trees, and highly-cultivated vicinage of the English castle, render it, independent of local history, the most characteristic object in the landscape. What the basilica is in Italy, the rampart of Vauban in France, and the pyramid in Egypt, is the castle in England — an architectural type and illustration of the primitive national life. Warwick Castle is the place to hear Shakspere's historical plays read by a fine elocutionist. Every allusion they contain finds a response in the scene. We feel there the old inspriation of chivalric days; Percy, Mortimer, Talbot, and Blount, become actualized in a spot so adapted to give scope to ambition, ferocity, and magnanimous valour; the use, abuse, origin, transition, maintenance, and bequest of power, are not only written in the annals, but inscribed on each mossy stone of the hoary pile; and reappear, blended with the artifices and expression of human nature, in her ever-identical instincts, as depicted by the great poet who translated the chronicles of his native land into vital dramas. We might infer his English origin by the term "cloud-capt" applied to tower, for it is a phenomenon almost peculiar to this climate; and as the cupola of St. Peter's gains new relief to the eye from the stainless azure against which it is so frequently seen, the less graceful but more warlike forms that rear themselves so proudly under Britain's lowering sky, borrow a more imposing grandeur from the detached masses of vapour that seem to cling around their dizzy summits.

Within the castle, amid so many suggestive relics and memorable effigies, although curiosity, at the time, is largely gratified, upon a few salient points of the whole array, does fancy linger in the retrospect; to me these were the chamber-furniture of Queen Anne, which, with her portrait by Sir Godfrey Kneller, over the mantel-piece, gives a singular unity of impression; the bust of Edward the Black Prince, Elizabeth's dagger, and the mask of Cromwell. The domestic appliances of the sovereign whose memory Marlborough and Addison linked with victory and verse, revived an epoch so diverse from that which lowered in the rugged and stern features of the dead Oliver, and was typified in the princely warrior of a knightly age, and the handsome weapon of the virgin queen, that each of these symbolic trophies recurred as talismans, evoking whole reigns from the buried past. Vandyke, Rubens, and other masters speak from the old walls in the precision of linear expression, or mellow richness of hue; and, at every step, we are tempted to linger and peruse the features of those who have suffered and triumphed in a manner that has made their names and fortunes household words in two hemispheres. What a story is associated with the Earl of Strafford; what a web of intrigue, extending over the world, with the astute, glowing, dignified, prayerful face of Ignatius Loyola; what pitiful interest environs the fair countenance of Charles I's queen; and how familiar appears Holbein's Henry VIII, the origin of his countless portraits. But earls and kings do not so harmoniously embody the ideal of history as the landscape, as fresh, though less wooded to-day, as when "the blue-eyed minstrel" strayed amid its oaks and elms. It was during a walk through the castle grounds, that the poetry of the scene come home to my heart. Weary with historical details, and warlike legends, it was refreshing to tread the elastic and twinkling grass, and see the old branches of noble trees wave in the gusty breeze. The symmetrical pines cast broad shadows; the few brown leaves that yet clung to the leafless oaks, were detached by the wind; birds were chirping; a banner fluttered from the tower; far away spread the clustered roofs of Warwick, and over them rose the old church pinnacles; looking upon these objects, as I strolled in the meadow, through which winds the Avon, two beautiful swans floated gracefully down the stream; and then I felt myself in a haunt of Shakspere. The castle, the town, the river, the queenly birds, each tree and grass-blade were rife with his gracious memory; and the murmurs of his harp seemed to vibrate in the wind, fragmentary snatches of historic and natural description. I looked at the old grey towers, and —

> "Saw young Henry with his beaver on,
> His cuisses on his thighs, gallantly armed,
> Rise from the ground like feathered Mercury."

I gazed at the sky, as the vapory rack consolidated in shifting and grotesque forms, and thought —

"Sometimes we see a cloud that's dragonish,
A towered citadel, a pendent rock,
A forked mountain, or blue promontory."

I paused beneath "the shade of melancholy boughs" and looked on the rough trunks for the name of Rosalind, and down the vistas, for Jacques prone on the sward in reverie; and with the legendary structure just visible through a leafy screen, asked myself is not —

"This life more sweet
Than that of painted pomp? Are not these woods
More free from peril than the envious court?"

A venerable keeper passed, and reminded me of good old Adam and the "constant service of the antique world," and a tanned loon in a field munching a turnip, had a Touchstone air. The famous vase named from this its grand depository, and the view from the highest tower, were also rife with interest. After winding through narrow passages, lofty saloons, and over oak floors all mellowed and worn by time, after tracing the antique carving round an enormous fire-place, that had consumed yule logs by thousands, gazed on ancient armour, reverend portraits, and, every now and then, through the vast window, upon the picturesque landscape, it was startling to my American sense of change, to see the gloves, hats, and overcoats, of the present occupants of Warwick Castle, lying on the hall-table. So completely had the manners and habiliments of a distant age occupied the mind, that this indication of hereditary proprietorship, of the absolute relation of living men to the old earls, came upon the senses as a miracle. To one who has lived in a country where it is rare to find the second generation beneath the same roof-tree, or to recognise a landmark after the lapse of twenty years, a land where change is the universal law, and vicissitude of fotune, locality, and employment almost the prevalent order of life, there is a positive sublimity in the spectacle of a home nine hundred years old; and I did not wonder at the spell of conservatism in a nation, where the family can gather, at Christmas in halls alive with traditions of ancestral barons, knights, and princes, sheltered from the winter air by tapestry, woven centuries ago, into the pictured exploits of warlike progenitors; and kneel to pray in a chapel, before whose altar have bowed a line of kindred extending from the origin of the kingdom to the present hour. To complete the expressive alternation of relics, in the lodge was a spider-legged table, at which Friar Tuck might have quaffed ale, and in the dining-room, an elaborately carved buffet, that had graced the World's Fair.

This bewildering combination of the past and present, so vivid at Warwick, vanishes at Kenilworth; there, instead of a complete and uninjured castle, we behold one in ruins; and, in felicity of position, in the grandeur of the fragments, and the whole environment of the scene, it is impossible to conceive architectural remains more poetically impressive. In these respects they are only equalled by the temples at Paestum, and the noble vestiges that stand in isolated majesty on the sea-washed cliff of Grigenti.

But the character of this ruin is essentially dissimilar, as thoroughly feudal as the others are Greek; and it is an extraordinary advantage, in a picturesque and meditative view, thus to behold a perfect structure, and one of the same species, in absolute ruins, within a few miles of each other. The leafy avenue you enter by a wicket, seems like a romantic passage from the immediate to antiquity; and the oak pannelling and sculptured fire-place of the old farm-house where you rest, memorials of the original edifice, whose foundation rise near, bring home the idea of the gorgeous interior of which no other trace remains.

It was with a thrill of awe and delight that, on a breezy morning, I stood amid the detached remnants of towers, walls, gateways, and windows grand in their proportions even in decay, and beheld the enormous root-branches of ivy whence clambered high and wide such a wilderness of foliage; and then, from the highest stand-point, gazed over a vast rural landscape, with meadows of intense green, dotted with large trees, and intersected by hedge-rows, here dark with new-ploughed fields, and there alive with grazing kine; and then turned again to clamber over broken steps of rock, into a massive dungeon, through some fissure in a battlement, up to a crumbling parapet, tracing the while, by means of a ground-plan, the site and relics of the gate-house and banqueting-room, the buildings of Leicester and Lancaster, the presence-chamber, the towers of Caesar, Mortimer, and Lun, King Harry's lodgings, Sir

Robert's lobby, and all the other localities, ever and anon saying to myself: "This is what time and rapine have spared of Kenilworth Castle!"

Near the beautiful stone frame-work of the lofty window hung so picturesquely with foliated garlands, I paused long and thoughtfully, to rebuild in fancy the broken walls, and repeople them with the great departed. I thought of Kenilworth in its prime, when beleagured by the hosts of Plantagenet, the witness of Edward II's captivity, and the triumph of Mortimer, the scene of John of Gaunt's revels, and Henry VIII's favourite abode. I recalled the era when it was the haunt of marauding followers of a rebellious earl, and when devastated by Cromwell's soldiers; but gradually these vague reminiscences settled into an animated picture of the festival which Leicester here dedicated to his queen. Not only have musty chroniclers, in the most quaint terms, recorded this memorable fête, but their details have been made to glow with life and unity of effect, in the pages of modern romance.

Again the country round seemed filled with purveyors, courtiers, and minstrels, on their way to the revels; again the sound of bugles echoed from the chase; morris-dancers were grouped on the lawn, knights in the tilt-yard, and fair ladies in the hall; before the "vestal throned in the west" plebeians knelt to rise up nobles, and scrofulous wretches quivered with delight beneath her healing touch; again the scutcheon of Geoffrey de Clinton glistened in the torch-light; Sussex scowled in rivalry on Leicester; plumes waved amid the trees, archers twanged their bows, an Italian tumbler leaped in the air, lovers whispered in a recess of the ball-room, an astrologer cast horoscopes in the tower, yeomen drank ale from huge flagons, and a pyrothenic glare revealed velvet doublets, flashing swords, and jewelled bosoms.

We who have so freshly in mind the creations of Scott, cannot avoid thinking chiefly, at Kenilworth, of Leicester and Elizabeth. At Warwick Castle I contemplated his portrait with interest; there was manly beauty and the dignity of high lineage in that face, but also a latent sternness of purpose in the mouth, and a sinister expression in the fine dark eye; it is the countenance of a handsome, proud, ambitious, and cruel man, and yet one capable of soft and high emotions. At his tomb in

St. Mary's Church, I also paused to gaze on the outstretched effigy, the same lineaments and costume as in the portrait, but less defined and more relieved; and now I stood amid the ruins of that princely abode, where royalty was his favoured guest, and mused upon his aspirations for the crown, of the Queen's attachment, of his intrigues, and especially of the long struggle of his heart between love and ambition. Here in the twilight, when the woman asserted herself in spite of the Queen, Elizabeth fondly whispered "Dudley!" and there, in the presence-chamber, when suspicion triumphed over confidence, she petulantly threatened, with an oath, to send him to the Tower. I thought of him driving the blood from Amy Robsart's delicate cheek, with the declaration: "The bear brooks no one to cross his awful path;" and wreathing the harsh features of Elizabeth into compacent smiles, by adroit flattery or glances of admiration.

This, according to tradition, was the window of the Queen's dressing-room: what reveries then may she not have indulged, in the rare intervals of self-communion permitted on that festal visit; how imperious will must have wrestled with passionate desire, and bitter jealousy poisoned her cup of luxury; she may have gazed hence upon the gallant form of her lover, as he sped forth on his steed, at dawn, to the hunt, and sighed as he disappeared in the forest, at her misgivings of his faith, or her sense of queenly prerogative that barred the realization of her tenderness.

With a lingering step and reverted gaze, after exploring the adjacent orchard, pleasaunce, and meadows, I left the ruins. The modern town of Kenilworth, and the ancient priory, a religious dependency of the castle in earlier times, were bathed in the mellow light of noon; thrushes sang in the hedge, sheep were clustered in the fields, and, as we followed a pleasant lane to the station, I asked myself, with the peerless bard:—

> "Gives not the hawthorne bush a sweeter shade
> To shepherds, looking on their silly sheep,
> Than doth a rich embroidered canopy
> To kings, that fear their subjects' treachery."

Shakspere was born at the epoch when these domestic and noble fortresses, with their dungeons and ramparts, were giving way to the handsome mansion reared in a peaceful meadow, with open porch, and only a rustic gate to separate it from the high-road. Thus the safety and amenities of later civilization were enjoyed by the bard, with those formidable structures of feudalism still undiminished, to make vivid the warlike, baronial past, and contrast its grim features with the serene cheerfulness of rural life. No period can be conceived more favourable to a free, bold, and creative imagination. A perverse steed, imposed on us at Warwick, by his capricious pauses on the road to Stratford, gave frequent opportunities for a survey of the country. Its aspect was fertile and agreeable, without being highly picturesque, and, by its very lack of prominent charms, led me to speculate upon the external resources of the poet. That subtle and pervasive element, which we familiarly call the spirit of the age, had more to do with his development than any rare scenery or local peculiarities; these he observed with wonderful accuracy; they yielded him details of still-life and shades of characterization; but, as far as the outward world influenced his creative faculty, the events and personages of his day, it may be justly inferred, were a prime incentive to that scope of argument and vital energy of perception which distinguish his genius.

To these scenes of quiet beauty and rural comfort he owes undoubtedly much of the tranquil grace of his Muse, much of the gentle patience of his tone, and not a little of the humane philosophy that so sweetly links the frailties and the pleasures of his race with the imagery of the natural world. Here he, "with an eye of leisure looked on all;" and bright are the traces in his plays, of that thoughtful communion with his native landscape: amid its sequestered loveliness, the tide of his soul moved calmly, reflecting every star in the heavens; but when it burst forth with the grand throes of the cataract, it was through contact with the stern events that thrilled his age, and under the iris-hued splendour of intellectual glory that spanned, like a prismatic bow, connecting earth and heaven, the valorous, experimental, prolific era of Elizabeth. The meagre facts of his individual culture furnish a most inadequate explanation of the mental phenomena included in his brief existence. When we have ascribed his classical knowledge, in part, to intimacy with Ben Johnson, traced his acquaintance with the old Italian romances, admitted the evidence that he owned a copy of Montaigne, and that the first English translation of "Plutarch's Lives" was coincident with his youth, there remains a vast body of special intelligence and a wide horizon of experience, which even his peerless endowment fails to explain.

The mystery, however, lessens when we take into view contemporary men and occurrences, and consider how full of significance they must have been to the thinker of that day. The most affecting historical episode, the life and martyrdom of Mary, Queen of Scots; the almost Arabian tales of maritime discovery which resulted in the settlement of America; the spiritual war, so long carried on with material weapons, that led to Protestantism in England; the glorious victories of Sir Francis Drake, and the heroic death of Sydney — were a few of the characteristic events of Shakspere's time. And, in purely intellectual experience, it was no less prolific: then the Puritan advent occured; Bacon philosophized; the Tower claimed some of its noblest victims; Titian painted; Spenser ushered forth the "Fairy Queen;" Hooker preached; Galileo read the stars; Cervantes "laughed Spain's chivalry away;" Tasso raved and sung; Inigo Jones built; Raleigh's friends were taught to smoke the Virginia weed; the Flemish exiles introduced manufactures into England; the earliest printing presses were put in motion; a wonderful galaxy of playwrights wheeled, like a new milky way, into the firmament of northern song, and substituted for the quaint old moralities an intensely human drama, which, in spite of its barbarisms, yet holds captive the Saxon heart. On such a flood of enterprise, thought, and incident, the matchless soul of WILLIAM SHAKSPERE was lifted into the empyrean; upon such a theatre was his wondrous insight expended; amid such glowing elements did his immortal genius expand and gradually mature into perfect achievement.

At Stratford-on-Avon, however, we are too much absorbed in the childhood, youth, and last days of Shakspere the man, to reflect long upon his age. It is the hazel eyes, the bald and lofty head, the auburn beard, the human figure that once moved through these streets, which haunt our fancy there; it is the stripling given "to poetry and acting," the glowing youth wooing, not a girl, but a woman parallel with his own thorough manliness, and therefore his senior, and "in the lusty stealth of

nature" taking the fair Anne Hathaway for his bride; it is the
spirited youth relishing a midnight shot in the forest, and
lampooning a complacent old squire — the rich autocrat of the
neighbourhood whom he was too independent to toady, and yet
not able wholly to defy: it is the romantic moonlight stroller,
upon whose fine sense not an odour, hue, or tone, was lost —
unconsciously garnering up, in this humble village, the material
elements of poetic creations destined "for all time;" and, finally,
it is the crowned minstrel, his eternal triumph achieved, his
glorious legacy to mankind enrolled, returning hither, in the
prime of life and fame, to celebrate his daughter's nuptials, make
his will, write his epitaph, dwell a while in grateful and meek
content, with kindred and neighbours, amid his sweet native
landscape, and then lay his body under the altar where in life he
prayed; — thenceforth to become a shrine of humanity, to
which his spirit, diffusive as the winds of heaven, and yet
concentrated as the heart's blood, shall draw the votive steps of
reverent and loving generations for ever!

Of all the claims upon faith to which the modern traveller is
liable, one of the most difficult not to admit, but to realize, is
that advanced by the sign projecting from the little cottage in
Henley Street, at Stratford. We tread the sagging floor, we gaze
round the low-roofed and diminutive chamber, we vainly seek
an unappropriated inch on wall and ceiling to inscribe our name,
we seat ourselves in the arm-chair, let the garrulous old woman
chatter away unheeded, and, all the time, there is a strife
between the senses and the mind, from the eagerness of the
latter to realize the identity of the scene with Shakspere's
nativity. But this troubled mood changes to one of happy
conviction, as we become familiar with the town itself and
adjacent country. It is easy to associate a poet with nature, and
very near seems he who first drew breath in yonder lowly
domicile, when streams, woods, insect, sky, and man himself,
are beheld where he first knew them. I could easily imagine here
the zest with which, glad to escape the more exciting lessons of
London life, he wrote:—

> "Often to our comfort, shall we find
> The sharded beetle in a safer hold
> Than is the full-winged eagle. O this life

> Is nobler than attending for a check,
> Prouder than rustling in unpaid-for silk."

At every step, his familiar phrase illustrated the scene. When we sat down to lunch at "The Red Horse," what better greeting could be imagined than —

> "May good digestion wait on appetite,
> And health on both!"

I looked out of the window, and there stood a venerable figure bent over his stick, his loose woollen hose betraying "the lean and slippered pantaloon;" there was no less than two infants "puling in their nurses' arms;" an urchin, playing ball, exhibited "the shining morning face" of the schoolboy; a blacksmith and currier were greedily swallowing news which a farmer ostentatiously broached; they were the "mechanic slaves with greasy aprons" of the play; under the window, stood an old toper, who methought sat for this picture: "There is a fellow somewhat near the door, for o' my conscience twenty dog-days now reign in's nose; all that stand about him are under the line;" a strutting groom was one of those inventoried by the same hand, as "highly fed and lowly taught;" a plethoric dame was arranging her newly-purchased stores in a cart, with the very expression of an "unlettered, small-knowing soul;" a bluff country-gentleman reined up his tall horse, as if to exhibit to the group his "fair, round belly, with good capon lined;" a lady's chariot outshone the whole array, and a carrier's waggon was an instant nucleus for gossips. It was essentially such a "walking shadow" of life as used to greet the eyes of the young poet. Indeed, I recognized, in an hour's walk about Stratford, a vast number of old acquaintances, especially Dogberry, Shallow, Snug, Bottom, and Launce's dog. But the most genial traces of his Muse are discoverable in natural objects. From Stratford to Shotely, his wife's maiden home, and thence to Charlecote, the seat of the deer-loving justice, how many silent testimonies to graphic pencil in the dramatic artist, strike the thoughtful eye!

The evidence of universal sympathy, so apparent in the pilgrimage of multitudes to a common shrine, attested the truth he so emphatically announced, that "one touch of nature makes the whole world kin;" his own marvellous destiny makes us feel that "there's a divinity that shapes our ends;" the headstones in the churchyard announce that "undiscovered country from whose bourne no traveller returns;" and thus each object and idea which the place suggested, whether by a detail of nature or a general truth, found its most apt expression in one of his memorable phrases.

The shrewd eye and obsequious bearing of an innkeeper made us exclaim, "How like a fawning publican he looks;" a discussion growing out of Queen Elizabeth's portraits, and the tales of her frailty, induced the charitable second thought to utter itself in his considerate line, "The greatest scandal waits on greatest state;" the complacent air of sanctity in a young and spruce vicar we met, suggested one of that class who believe there shall be "no more cakes and ale" because they are virtuous; and hastening at sunset along the road to Warwick, we could say —

> "The west yet glimmers with some streaks of day,
> Now spurs the lated traveller apace
> To gain the timely inn."

Here, I thought, when love "lent a precious seeing to the eye," Shakspere beheld the landscape now present to my vision; speeding with full heart to his tryst at eve, "the sweet odour of the new-mown hay" breathed its fragrance around him; "violets dim" met his downward glance; "the poor beetle that we tread upon," crossed his path; the willow that "shows its hoar leaves in the glassy stream" became a pensive image in his memory; "the barky fingers of the elm" touched his flushed brow; the umbrageous fence that skirted his way, years after, led him to write, "Such a divinity doth *hedge* a king;" he saw the cheerful rustic coming home from toil, and knew, when in the great world, how blest it is "to range with humble livers in content;" the decrepit villagers that hobbled by, taught him that "Care keeps his watch in every old man's eye;" the echo of the funeral-bell impressed upon his thought that "we cannot hold mortality's strong hand;" and though convivially inclined when "fancy free," he left the alehouse early where there was "like to be a great presence of worthies," breaking away from the bore "full of wise saws and modern instances;" and, as these casual experiences took their place in the background of the temple of his mind, he thus inwardly ejaculated:—

> "O, that I thought it could be in a woman

> To feed for aye her lamp and flames of love;
> To keep her constancy in plight and youth,
> Outliving beauty's outward, with a mind
> That doth renew swifter than blood decays!
> Or, that persuasion could but thus convince me,
> That my integrity and truth to you
> Might be affronted with the watch and weight
> Of such a winnowed purity in love;
> How were I then uplifted!"

He heard, as he walked, the "brook make music with the enamelled stones," and saw the river "giving a gentle kiss to every sedge," even as they do now; and, at the same time, speculating on his own consciousness, he thought —

> "O, how this spring of love resembleth
>   The uncertain glory of an April day,
> Which now shows all the beauty of the sun,
>   And by-and-by a cloud takes all away!"

After the limitless flight of a sympathetic imagination through the natural, historical, ideal, and human world created by Shakspere, what an appeal to our humanity is his tomb! As, beneath a wintry sky, I walked up the avenue of old trees to the church where he is buried the fitful blast rose and died away in the mossy boughs like a perpetual requiem. The dark evergreen and the dry limbs, the head-stones and turf, the cloud-shadows alternating over the broken pavement, joint emblems of Nature's constant renewal, and of Death's oblivious mystery, familiar as they were, had, then and there, an utterance of awe and beauty. The quiet venerable church, thus isolated from the thickly-settled part of the town, and embowered in foliage, with its truly English aspect and religious seclusion, was quite in accordance with the mood awakened by the presence of its concentrated dust.

How noble in its simplicity was the image of the great bard, in his domestic character, kneeling there in prayer beside wife, daughter, and grandchild; holding meekly, in his Creator's presence, the sublime faculties which, with all their heritage of power and of fame, could not exempt him from a single infirmity "that flesh is heir to." The improvidence and vagrant habits of genius are proverbial; self-respect and loyalty to social duty, are rare in the career of the gifted; and to my mind there was something inexpressibly affecting in the evidence here given of Shakspere's careful regard for his own and his family's sculpture. To come back in the zenith of his dramatic success and the vigour of his years, to the village whence he wandered in youth, to arrange his affairs, regulate the disposition of his property, and provide a last resting-place for his dust, guarding it, by a benediction and a curse, from profanation, was a phase of forethought and consideration, in contrast with his unequalled intellectual triumphs, that seemed to me full of moral significance.

The gentleman of Stratford-on-Avon was not allowed to disappear in the glory of the poet of all time. When the good clerk of the parish rolled off a long strip of matting from before the altar-railing, and disclosed the inscribed slabs which cover his bones and those of his wife and daughters, I thrilled with reverence at the possible destiny of a man: here was the ocular proof of his mortality, of his experience of the common lot; but the hushed expanse of that country church, "in my mind's eye," was thronged with the brave, the fair, and the gifted, who sprang into ever-fresh and cherished being at his call. Think of our inward life, bereft of these! Could we not muse with Hamlet, drink the honey vows of Romeo, find majesty in woe with Lear, realize the omnipresence of conscience in the visions of Macbeth and Richard, and quicken faith in woman in the society of Miranda, Cordelia, Juliet and Hermione — how faint would be the recorded types of humanity, how vague our ideals of the race! And these passions that rend our hearts, the dark annals that men call history, the scenes of Nature, and the philosophy of life — imagine them without the key of this master-spirit, the consolations, beauty, tenderness, and truth, with which he has reconciled "the show of things to the desires of the mind."

The church was dressed with spruce and holly, and round the bust of Shakspere, above his epitaph, sprigs of bay were twined. The cheerful hue of those polished leaves seemed to proclaim the eternal freshness of his memory. The authenticity of this bust is undeniable, and its expression is a blended intelligence and kindliness; intellect — high, self-possessed, and clear — and habitual benignity, were the characteristics of his face. A more serene and noble countenance, grand in its outline, and gentle in its spirit, cannot be imagined. The subdued calm and holy light of the temple breathed of peace. The desolation of mortality vanished in thoughts of the undying love and honour which consecrate his fame. He has told us, with a humility and affection unparalleled in the personal utterance of genius, how he would have one that loved him feel beside his tomb:–

> "No longer mourn for me when I am dead,
> Than you shall hear the surly sullen bell
> Give warning to the world that I am fled
> From this vile world with vilest worms to dwell:
> Nay, if you read this line, remember not
> The hand that writ it; for I love you so,
> That I in your sweet thoughts would be forgot
> If thinking on me then should make you wo.
> O if, I say, you look upon this verse
> When I perhaps compounded am with clay,
> Do not so much as my poor name rehearse,
> But let your love with my poor life decay;
> Lest the wise world should look into your moan,
> And mock you with me after I am gone."

CHAPTER IX

BY THE WAY

> To know
> That which before us lies in daily life,
> Is the prime wisdom.

MILTON

De Quincey tells us that his first childish impressions of the magnitude of London, was derived from the sight of the immense droves of cattle in the suburban roads, all tending to one point, and destined to supply the metropolitan markets; and Dr. Johnson perambulated the streets forty years before he encountered an old Derbyshire friend, whose diurnal walks embraced the same circle; but the stranger now gains the most vivid idea of this vastness, after a day passed amid the luxurious dwellings of the West End, by a nocturnal pilgrimage through the most crowded thoroughfares of the city; on Saturday evening they swarm with shopkeepers, clerks, porters, dandies, errand-boys, women, and mechanics, and as one adroitly threads the long procession, the strong artificial light falls on wan or burly faces, and helps to increase the panoramic effect; the blue and orange reflection of the chemist's bottles, alternate with red quarters of beef and enormous cabbages; we pass in rapid succession, the Chinese effigies of a tea-shop, the gloomy materials of the undertaker; here a surgeon's name emblazoned on metal, and there piles of clothing or rows of shoes, pyramids of candy, folds of gay silk, masses of dried fruit, a book-stall covered with faded volumes, miserable little exhibitions, "dissolving views," "exhilarating gas," and "concerts," allurements to resorts for drinking; all revealed in the blaze of innumerable gaslights, and presided over by stiff policemen,

with dreadnought coats and glazed hats. The scene calls to mind
the observation of a French traveller, who says England is "Un
pays rempli de gens qui ne demandent pas mieux que d'échanger
un schilling contre une émotion de deux minutes."

Mayhew has given us the diagnosis of London street-life, with
an analytical precision quite scientific. By means of statistics
carefully gleaned, daguerreotype portraits of each species of
huckster, and descriptions authentic and detailed, a body of the
most curious information is brought together, which reveals a
world of facts, appalling to the sensibilities, and wonderfully

suggestive to the political economist. After reading "London Labour and London Poor," it is impossible to note the coster-mongers, and recognize the by-way tableaux, without emotion.

Having been charged, before leaving home, with a missive to a celebrated political refugee, I sought his obscure domicile, through more than a league of crowded streets, and during the transit from Tafalgar Square to King's Road, the situation of a foreigner, and especially that of a poor exile from Southern Europe, in this wilderness of human beings, presented itself in tragic relief. I thought of the melancholy charm we all learned to associate with it, before the vein opened by "Thaddeus of Warsaw" had been exhausted by later novelists.

In a gloomy court, on the edge of one of those highways always thronged with beeves and coal-drays, and illuminated at night by the flashing and fatal gin-palaces, I found, after many inquiries, the mean abode where dwelt one, who, but a few months previous, had swayed a popular conclave, and repre-sented an awakened and exultant nation. The slatternly hostess scrutinized and hesitated before she admitted me to the patriot's chamber. The remains of a meagre breakfast lay on the deal table, which was heaped with the tobacco-stained files of a liberal journal in a foreign tongue; lithographs of republican leaders hung awry on the wall; everything betokened impover-ished seclusion, uncheered save by memory and hope.

Isolated in a vast metropolis, the mercurial child of the South thus lived, safe, indeed, from *gens d'armes,* but deprived of all that endears life, except the mere privilege of living; his only excitement obtainable from journals and letters, those charts of action and love to the banished; incapable of adaptation to the people and habits around, with hearts embittered by ceaseless regret, and forlorn though unshared aspirations, these victims of despotism experience hourly alternate pangs and desires, whose conflict might melt a stoic with pity.

What a contrast is the scene on which their fevered eyes open to that of home! The blue sky, the radiant sunshine, the music, statues, ruins, and flowers, which endear their native land for ever, even to the passing stranger, here only mock the imagin-ation with a vanished dream. The traffic, fog, and hubbub of pitiless London whirl around their hearts like a vision of despair. How many noble spirits have tasted this bitter cup, whose names are identified with intellectual triumphs, or social virtues worthy a happier destiny. I thought of Kosciusko and the days of enthusiasm for Poland, yet alive in the spirited verse of Campbell; of the gentle lexicographer Baretti, and the Corsican hero, Paoli, companioned by Johnson; of romaneque Chateaubriand teaching French, and writing in a garret for bread, of Foscolo with his sybarite tastes, and elegiac muse, of Mazzini and Kossuth; the spasmodic outbreaks of popular sympathy, and the reaction into indifference and ridicule; and I felt how utterly vain was the attempt to harmonize Southern instincts with English pride, the enthusiasm of a vivacious, with the rationality of a phlegmatic race. The foreigner is ever apart in London; if he is seen a night or two in a fashionable assembly, or is made to figure in a political ovation, his very complexion, eye, and bearing, emphatically declare him alien to the scene. His rhetorical speech, visionary tone of mind, childlike sensitiveness, and extravagant manner, have a grotesque prominence amid the systematic respectability, and cold self-possession of the people who give him refuge.

The Teutonic exiles alone reconcile themselves patiently to English life; Freiligrath, the beautiful lyrist of freedom, is bravely content to support his family by keeping the books of a London merchant; but Mazzini roams, with fiery eyes, amid the uncongenial throng, or shuts himself up, for weeks, in an obscure lodging, to indite constitutional formulas, or sententious appeals. An Englishman cannot imagine the desolation which a child of the South feels from the absence of the sun, and the presence of an exclusively utilitarian life; even the comfortable proprieties of an English home fail to solace their eager spirits; Corinne's picture, however melo-dramatic in design, is essentially true in spirit. England nobly gives an asylum to the life, but not to the soul of the refugee; she is, with casual exceptions, true to national hospitality; but it is the aegis of her laws, and not the embrace of her sympathy, which she casts around the hunted stranger.

In fact, the chivalric element, in its legitimate influence, is not native to English blood; animal courage, loyalty, and frank kindness to those who have a claim on their protection, are, indeed, characteristic and noble traits; but the sympathetic, trustful, voluntary heart of courtesy, is a different and a rare virtue.

Women, for instance, as such, feel sensibly the inferiority of their position; the voluntary aid and habitual deference they receive, merely on the score of their sex, in America, is not vouchsafed in England. The discontent manifested by women in this country, who advocate special rights would be diminished, if they could realize the comparative absence of respect and sympathy experienced abroad.

It is far more common than with us, among the professional and mercantile class in England, to retire at middle age upon a competency; and nothing can be more pleasing to a wise and generous nature than to behold the peaceful evening which thus succeeded to the busy noon of life. To an American especially it is delightful to see contented and well-earned leisure embellished by useful taste and hallowed by domestic virtue. I sought, one afternoon, the house of a retired physician, the only surviving London contemporary of a medical friend at home, whom I had promised to report to his old fellow-student. To this kindly and intelligent gentleman I should not personally refer, but a literary enterprise that has beguiled several years of his retirement, is about to benefit transatlantic readers; and this circumstance is an adequate reason for infringing upon the grateful silence, in regard to private intercourse, which should chasten every honourable traveller's record. I accompanied Dr. Roget to a meeting of the Royal Society. A paper, abounding in curious facts, was read on "The transmission of Heat;" but while I mechanically listened to the scientific thesis, my eye wandered reverentially to the portraits of Evelyn, Sir Joseph Banks, John Hunter, Dr. Baillie, Franklin, and others, that adorned the walls, to the bust of Carlo II, fondator, to the golden mace, and the faces of the members; and, upon adjourning to the library, there were relics that carried me yet farther from the immediate discussion — the telescope constructed by Sir Isaac Newton, his likeness, mask taken after death, a lock of his hair, and a striking bust of Mrs. Somerville.

Dr. Roget was, for twenty years, secretary of the Royal Society; his work to which I have referred is a kind of verbal anatomy, a collection of English synonyms arranged with reference to their shades of meaning, and the needs of the student. It may be called a philosophical vocabulary. All who have a vivid sense of language, who aim at exactness of speech, and to whom writing is a high art, are familiar with the difficulty of seizing the precise word to express the desired sentiment or idea. Our ideal in this regard is often sacrificed to the caprice of memory. For this and many other wants of the mind, in its relation to language, "Roget's Thesaurus" will prove an invaluable manual. He has made an analytical study of our vernacular, traced the origin and ramification of words, arrayed their elemental forms in rational order, and thus furnished a kind of verbal scale, by which we can harmonize and emphasize our language to the utmost nicety and greatest significance.

The conservative habit of the English is very obvious to an American eye, in the physique, the costume, and even in the mechanic arts and trades around him. It is not surprising that an Englishman, newly arrived in Boston, thought himself among a nation of invalids; the pedestrian activity of the women, and their apparent indifference to the elements, and the number of robust, old men on the promenades, in London, are novelties to us. I found a celebrated watchmaker playing cribbage, one evening, with his wife, in a plain, old-fashioned house of Clerkenwell, where not an indication appeared of his auriferous vocation, or the fame and activity whereby he and his fathers before him, had so long there prospered.

An industrial nation, like England, naturally makes greater provision for science than art; and the list of public benefactors in this department, with the immortal Newton at its head, and such men as Banks for purveyor, and Watt, Davy, Herschell, Priestly, Brewster, and other discoverers, so admirably delineated by Lord Brougham, to illustrate the annals of the Royal Society, is unique, while the British Museum, Zoological Gardens, Museum of Geology, and kindred institutions, afford the most abundant means for its permanent increase. The magnificent halls, completeness of each branch, and excellent arrangements of the former institution, the well-behaved crowds of visitors, gratified poor, busy artists, and absorbed students, rendered this, to my mind, the most obviously efficient of the London resorts, as well the noblest temple of knowledge. Nor is the superiority of the Zoological Gardens over similar establishments less apparent. I was struck with the number of small native birds, that frequent the place; are they attracted by the foreign individuals of their kind, or the chance of obtaining

food? It is pleasing to note how comfortably the exiles from desert, sea, and woods, are here domiciled; to watch the iris-hued waterfowl, brilliantly-scaled reptiles, gaudy parrots, flexible monkeys, and fierce hyenas; the opportunity to observe every species of animal tribes and feathered races, is so commodious, that it alone induces a taste for natural history; the authenticity of the comparison, "fat as a seal," was demonstrated here, as I watched a sleek and tame one, whose skin appeared filled to its utmost dimensions, run and dive, like a dog, for the silvery fish thrown by the keeper. The great rarity, however, was the hippopotamus, who had figured so often in "The Illustrated News," that he looked like an old acquaintance; and brought to mind the reedy margin of the White Nile, where he was captured when a few days old, by a huntsman, the scar of whose spear is still visible.

A note of introduction from Sir Charles Lyell obtained an item of practical information of which I was in quest, from the secretary of the Museum of Geology. The exquisitely-veined marbles and rare specimens of mineralogy there, might usefully occupy hours even to the unscientific; and the newly appreciated resources of Australia, were made evident by some large diamonds, and a lump of gold embedded in quartz, that rivalled the finest Californian specimens.

An opportunity was afforded me of thoroughly observing an old-school merchant. He was an epitome of John Bull in the average phase — a well-knit frame, a ruddy and clean-shaved chin, every article of his dress adapted to the existent weather, and indicative of entire comfort, but in neither cut nor hue giving the slightest hint of taste; neat, reserved, and civil; his opinions based on extreme rationality, without impulse, systematic in exercise and diet, self-reliant, scrupulous in asserting his nationality, in his salutations, his promenade, his reading, his conservative dogmas in politics, and his audible responses to the Church Service; frank and kind in his hospitality, complacent, wedded to decorum, balanced accounts, the Liturgy, and "The Times;" his port, sirloin, Cheshire, muffins, tea, servants, door-plate, finger-nails, creed, and wife, quite unexceptionable; — he was a human machine well oiled, in the highest working condition, a model of punctuality, good faith, health, and self-esteem — the creature of habit, and the incarnation of respectability.

The vast difference in the number of readers in America and England, may be inferred from the high price and limited editions of British journals, and the suggestive fact that out of London, not a single daily newspaper is issued, while the penny press is almost unknown. The new works forwarded to the nobility, may be seen, months after their publication, with uncut leaves, on the library tables. Poetry is far less read; Tennyson and the Brownings have a hundred American to one English admirer; and until Dickens established "Household Words," but few periodicals reached the masses in which reliable information was diffused at a price and with the graces of style requisite for its general usefulness. The essays of Carlyle, Macaulay, De Quincey, and other valuable contributors to British periodical literature, were first collected on this side of the water.

I was desirous to compare the successors of Curl, Evans, and Dodsley, with their famous predecessors in trade. To us accustomed to think of an English publisher's imprint as the sign-manual prophetic of intellectual luxury, the establishments whence our favourite books have emanated, are quite different from the idea formed of them. Instead of the gay shelves and large, frequented, and well-stocked warehouse, familiar to the bibliopole in American cities, we usually find a dusky office with a meagre array of specimen copies; the autocrat of the famous press occupies a back or upper parlour, and looks more like an author than a bookseller; the Longmans, adepts in publishing enterprise; Murray, with his celebrated portraits, and heritage of famous literary correspondence; Moxon in his retired sanctum, the author of a volume of sonnets; Bohn, a German scholar, surrounded by a multifarious and rare library; Bentley, by his cosy fireside, an acknowledged judge of style, originality, and the wants of the literary public; Pickering, in his suit of black, a lover of meditative genius, and a connoisseur in editions — all, by their environment and aspect, give one the idea of men of letters instead of traders; and so, to a greater or less extent, they are.

Comparatively speaking, books in England are a luxury; and those who publish standard works, abound in literary anecdote, cultivate special tastes, and minister, with no little social *éclat*, or *dilettante* instinct, at the altar of knowledge and mental enjoyment. There is little or no display in their places of business, which usually have a conservative and domestic, and seldom a busy look. Some devote their attention exclusively to the distribution of a few valuable works; others are identified with a single class of publications; and all, who have an established reputation, obviously depend upon the fame of their respective issues, and the certainty of demand, and not upon the allurements of conventional devices. I found these gentlemen, from their intimate relations with endeared authors, and practical knowledge of public taste, worthy purveyors in the field of literature; scarcely one but could relate a curious illustration of pencraft or character, that would have been seized upon by Disraeli the elder; and in the way of success, failure, rival editions, and the latent facts of the book-trade, their experience furnished abundant material equally interesting to the amateur and the economist.

Cheap literature is yet a novelty in England; it properly began with the railway libraries: and one distadvantage under which our authors, of the higher class, labour, in the absence of an international copyright, is that of having their books printed in so shabby and imperfect a style, that they rarely come under the eye of the cultivated readers for whom they were intended.

A signal advantage which the English author enjoys, is that, when once his ability is recognised, his publishers foster his genius. The successful career of many popular writers of the day is traceable, in no small degree, to the loyal and permanent encouragement they receive from the individual of the trade who becomes their medium, with the public; a foot-hold once deservedly gained, may thus be permanently lucrative; and what originated in a casual impulse or urgent necessity, lead to long and brilliant triumphs. The days seem to have gone by when a new poem created a *furore,* and a fresh review a panic; but the dinner, that great central point of demonstration in all branches of social interest, literary, dramatic, and artistic, according to the very genius of English life, has the same hospitable significance as when Moore enlivened it with his songs, Hook with unique imitations, and Sydney Smith with humerous sallies.

Diverse as are the forms of government in England from our own, there is one feature of politics in which they agree; the emphasis of the gazettes is entirely disproportioned to the public sympathy in questions of the day; even a change of ministry is far more prominent in the journals than as a matter of fact; and the reason of this comparative indifference is identical in both nations; — faith in constitutional safeguards, and the essential healthfulness of popular sentiment.

With all the benefits of the acoustic principle, and other modern improvements in the new House of Commons, we miss the associations of old St. Stephen's, as the scene of that grand intellectual gladiatorship between Pitt and Fox, the traditional eloquence of Sheridan, and the philosophic rhetoric of Burke. The scene where revolutions of opinion have been achieved, such as affect the destiny of nations, is hallowed to the mind; and the very walls that echoed the proud contempt of Pitt, and the vital argument of Fox, in that era when reckless dissipation alternated with momentous exhibitions of party tactics and oratory, have no little interest to an American, as witnesses of the councils that stimulated his country into an independent political existence; and as the arena where the talent most universal there, displayed its standard exemplars.

The Dutch painters excel in what we technically called interiors, their aptitude finding a scope therein which the unpicturesque landscape of their country denies; and, on the same principle, whoever would estimate life in England must seek its domestic manifestations. I had the curiosity to note what struck me as characteristic, during my visits of business and friendship in London; and, in every intance, recognized abundant material for philosophic inference. In no modern city is the diversity and permanence of the forms of social existence, more obvious. The sources whence the old dramatists, the modern essayists, and the writers of fiction of our own day, derive both their still-life, and their characters, are at once apparent; and the influences that mould the English mind, are seen to be of that reserved kind, which are born of household vocation and caste.

It is interesting, also, to trace the effect of science in modifying the conditions of life, and the amelioration which progressive elements have wrought in the social economy. These are more evident in the ratio of the intellectual quality of each occupaion; trade favours the monotony born of systematic routine; the bankers and artificers work in the same dens as they did a century ago; but professional men, and especially authors, have risen in the scale of civil life. Instead of Otway choking from the bread too late and too fiercely seized, we have Dickens substantially housed, and, with business-like method, sending forth his monthly number, which coins as reliable a pile of guineas, as any won by artizan or trader. Instead of the Court verifier anxious for his pittance, we have Barry Cornwall inditing a song, as he rides to attend a commission of lunacy; livelihood being quite independent of the Muse.

The contradictions of the English character are proverbial, and it is absurd to refer them to a single cause. Madame de Staël says, that when we are much attached to our ideas, we endeavour to connect everything to them; and the government, climate, and insular position of England, fail to explain any but general traits; it would be as irrational to ascribe the utilitarianism of the people, for instance, to a limited monarchy, as it was in De Tocqueville to derive so many American characteristics exclusively from the democratic principal.

That labour is peculiarly requisite to health and enjoyment, in a land affording so few natural resources in the way of luxury, is, indeed, obvious; and, not many years ago, the number of retired country gentlemen who died of apoplexy, was an alarming evidence of the danger of idleness, combined with a diet of beef, port, and ale. The last winter was wet and gloomy beyond all precedent, and more railway accidents then occurred than ever before in the same period, yet it struck me as a bold speculation to attribute these to an indifference to life, induced by the spleen consequent on so many weeks of rain. The complication of agencies that here bear upon, and modify human life, as well as the limited arena, and fixed destiny of humanity, render England, however, a far less favourable country for the study of social science than our own; insular communities are essentially peculiar; and the heritage of laws, customs, and ranks, that weight on the old nations, pervert, as well as narrow the development of each successive generation.

There are facts in the history of English civilization, which are reliable exponents of national character. The vital necessity of self-reliance, and of working out the problem of life to its most intense degree, which is the natural consequence of limited space, few external resources, and a northern atmosphere and organization, doubtless, in a great measure, account for the vast foreign empire, and concentrated industrial energy of the nation. These circumstances, too, generate a love of power, which habit renders a normal function of character; and hence it is, that Will is the predominant element, and that the English, like a tree, strike deep roots in the soil, and spread forth large branches to inhale their vitality from abroad, in order to grow strong by intense and gradual absorption, rather than bloom, like the flower, in evanescent grace, as the nations of the South and the East.

This vital energy, this perverse individuality, whether exhibited in reserve of manner, patience in action, or habitual arrogance, is the one prevailing and self-preserving instinct of the race; it is evident in the firm purpose of Wellington, the dogged industry of Johnson, the scornful defiance of Pitt, the bullyism of Thurlow, the assumption of Warren Hastings, the unflinching hardihood of English sailors, merchants, warriors, and authors. It is a personification of the voluntary principle, and the basis of the favourite character of obstinate old gentlemen, wilful youths, courageous soldiers, martyrs to opinion, and perverse women, so familiar to the reader of English literature. It is the instinctive cause of the national appellative; a bull is the animal type of strength, ferocity, and self-will.

In the American character these traits are modified by superior flexibility and greater aptness and variety. On the continent, while an Englishman remains intact, an American yields himself somewhat to the life he encounters; and the diversity is obvious in the national career of each. John Bull is content with the old as long as his personal comfort is not invaded; Jonathan is never so pleased but he is willing to do better; the one, therefore, is habitually conservative, the other experimental; and, as a consequence, the English excel in permanent resources, and the Americans in casual expedients; the one is better entrenched, the other commands a wider outlook; the one relies more steadily, the other invents with greater facility; and hence, in cases of mutual interest, they often work into each other's hands with effective skill, and to desirable results; but the idiosyncrasy of each is wholly diverse, tending, in the one case, to concentrate and individualize resources and aims, and, in the other, to diffuse and vary them.

The two poles of English life are unsociability and domesticity — representing the positive and negative elements; the spirit of trade quells the zest for amusement, and, by attaching a price to everything, induces an over-estimate of wealth, and makes poverty almost a crime; common sense and habits of industry are the useful but unaspiring standard of action; and when free of this normal condition, the English mind becomes splenetic, and exhibits the symptoms so eloquently displayed in Byron's verse. Then John Bull wishes a cause to die for — if neither the Exchange, the Admiralty, the War-office, nor the Club, bring solace to the misanthropy of leisure, and there is no home upon which to fall back in sullen dignity.

"Punch" has discovered a burlesque emblem for all nationalities. The most appropriate for England, at least under her winter aspect, would be a tea-kettle and an umbrella — one being the universal in-door cordial, and the other the great external necessity of the climate. The traces of "merry England" it is difficult to find; her cottage-homes exist mainly in poetry; races and elections now comprise her festivals, and this is doubtless the result of the steady encroachment of trade and manufactures upon agricultural life.

With a foreigner for his companion, when travelling in England, an American soon becomes aware of the greater intimacy of relation which he enjoys with the past and present of the country. No infantile reminiscence, musical with nursery-rhymes, startles the Frenchman beside you, when the guard bawls at the carriage-window, "Banbury Cross;" the German friend, on whose arm you lean, walking through Holborn, does not pause instinctively, as if his boot-nails were glued to the pavement by a magnet, at the sight of Day and Martins's sign; and the Italian, full of patriotic memories of Canova, wonders at you in St. Paul's, for standing so long before Abercrombie's monument, ignorant as he is, that the position of the dying general taught Kean how to fall naturally in his tragic death-scenes. An hour by "Shrewsbury clock" is no more significant to a continental than that noted by any other dial; he will scarcely think at Bath of Frances Burney, Jane Austen, or Smollet; or of Coleridge, Southey, and Wordworth, at Bristol. The cliff at Dover to his eyes is only an abrupt elevation of jagged chalk; no blind Glo'ster stands on the ledge, nor samphire gleaner, midway down, follows his "dreadful trade."

It is from our sympathy with the mind of the country that her landscape often wears an occult charm. We have an *à priori* attachment to London because the soul of Shakspere encamped so long in its midst. To us, England is the land where Wordsworth, with heroic love and patience, waited at the pure altar he had built to Nature and the Muses; where Carlyle, with his logical hammer, knocked away the flimsy incrustations with which hypocrisy and conventionalism shroud reality, and vindicated the essential and true in life and man; where Mrs. Hemans sung of home; Miss Edgeworth applied the test of sense and prudence to social life; Shelley kindled into aerial fantasy the dreams of classicism and reform; Bentham benignly advocated the greatest good of the greatest number; Macaulay made brilliant rhetorical digests; and Hood sent forth lyrics and puns alike provocative to tears of mirth and pity. When vexed by her arrogance, therefore, or restless under the vast shadow of her civic power, we find, in the thought of intellectual obligation and kindred, a constant antidote for the bane.

The national characteristics of the English prove, upon personal experience, to be derived from extremes; and hence the apparent inconsistency of prejudice and praise bestowed on them by foreign writers. Hospitality, for instance, is a proverbial trait; but he who imagines that this virtue springs from a rare facilty of intercourse, and a voluntary extension of kindness, will be greatly disappointed. The French and Italians far excel their insular neighbours in outward and ready courtesy. It is the quality and not the universality of this noble trait, that has given England her fame as its legitimate exponent. The access to her domestic sanctuaries is jealously guarded; but once opened, the confidence, freedom, and heartiness, are entire. Nowhere do the arrangements of private life so aptly fit the needs of the stranger; in no dwellings is he sooner made unconscious of that name; and the consequence is, that two quite distinct impressions are borne away from England; one critical, and relating to the country as a whole, to the idea of the nation in the abstract; and the other a sentiment of grateful attachment and of high respect toward individuals, families, and friends — than which no reminiscence of travel can be more permanent and earnest.

THE END